Cookery for Seamen

First edition published in 1894 by Tinling and Co. Printers.
This edition published in 2019 by the National Maritime Museum,
Park Row, Greenwich, London SE10 9NF.

ISBN: 978-1-906367-62-6

At the heart of the UNESCO World Heritage Site of Maritime Greenwich are
the four world-class attractions of Royal Museums Greenwich – the National
Maritime Museum, the Royal Observatory, the Queen's House and *Cutty Sark*.

www.rmg.co.uk

A CIP catalogue record for this book is available from the British Library.

Designed by Ocky Murray
Printed and bound in the UK by Gomer Press

10 9 8 7 6 5 4 3 2 1

Created from an original copy of *Cookery for Seamen* currently stored in the
Caird Library and Archive (PBE0303)

The Caird Library and Archive at the National Maritime Museum is the
most extensive maritime reference resource in the world. Available to anyone
interested in maritime history, items can be accessed for free online or in
person, all that is required is to register for a Reader's Ticket. Please contact
library@rmg.co.uk for more information.

The publisher or authors cannot be held responsible for any illness or injury
incurred by replicating any of the recipes or activities in this book. Caution
should be taken if attempting any cooking procedures that may not fall in line
with modern safety practices.

CONTENTS

INTRODUCTION

THIS POCKET-SIZE COOKERY book, which was first published
in 1894, is a facsimile of one in the collection of the National
Maritime Museum's Caird Library. It provides us with a
porthole-view into the diet of crew and passengers near the end
of Queen Victoria's reign. Some items on the menu are familiar
to us today. These include tomato soup, fish cakes, roast beef,
toad in the hole, Bakewell pudding and blancmange. Others are
less familiar! If you want to know how to cook sheep's tongue
in aspic, sheep's head broth or bullock's heart, then the answers
are to be found in the pages of this volume.

The book's authors were both involved in the teaching of
cookery skills to seamen. Liverpudlian Alexander Quinlan was
a ship's cook who was recruited to teach cookery to seamen in
classes provided by Liverpool City Council. Miss N.E. Mann
was the head teacher at the Liverpool Training School of
Cookery. The school, which was later the F.L. Calder College of
Domestic Economy, had been founded by Fanny Louisa Calder
back in 1875. Originally for female students, it later opened its
doors to males. Classes for ships' cooks began in 1891.

Though cooks purchased some provisions in port, at this period
a ready supply of fresh meat was carried by vessels in the form
of live animals which varied in size from poultry to cattle. The
cook's role extended to caring for this on-board farm, as well as
(in some cases) slaughtering and butchering the animals. Thus it
is that *Cookery for Seamen* includes details of how to do this.

Ships' cooks therefore required a wider set of skills than those
essential for the kitchen alone. Add to this the difficulties of

preparing meals in a confined space, with restricted ingredients, on board a moving vessel in all weather conditions, and the cook's role was indeed a challenging one. Since the cook was responsible for feeding everyone on board, no matter what their rank or station, they were also responsible in no small degree for the health and morale of the crew and passengers.

It was common for publications at this period to include advertisements and the original edition of *Cookery for Seamen* was no exception. In order to give a flavour of the original, reproductions of some of the advertisements have been included at the end of this facsimile. Can you spot the recommendation from one of the book's authors?

Though cooks were often reviled, their importance was starting to be recognised by the time *Cookery for Seamen* first appeared. Mann and Quinlan had been providing cookery classes for seamen since 1891 and 1892 respectively, and 1893 saw the establishment of the London School of Nautical Cookery. The next decade would see the introduction of certificates of competency for cooks in the merchant service, meaning that cooks had to be formally qualified.

Let us, then, vicariously sample the fare of the late Victorian ship's cook. Why not go a stage further and try some of the recipes in your own kitchen, be it on land or at sea?

Stawell Heard
Librarian, National Maritime Museum

COOKERY FOR SEAMEN,

— BY —

ALEXANDER QUINLAN,

Teacher of the Liverpool City Council Seamen's Cookery Classes,

AND

N. E. MANN,

Head Teacher of the Liverpool Training School of Cookery.

Issued under the direction of the Committee of the Liverpool Training School of Cookery.

PRICE, SIXPENCE.

LIVERPOOL:
C. TINLING AND CO., PRINTERS, VICTORIA STREET.
1894.

LIVERPOOL CITY COUNCIL

TECHNICAL EDUCATION COOKERY CLASSES FOR SEAMEN,

CONDUCTED BY THE

Liverpool Training School of Cookery

WITH THE CO-OPERATION OF THE

Liverpool Shipowners' Association.

L ESSONS IN COOKERY of the articles usually provided for Seamen are being given daily, from 10 a.m. to 12 noon and 2 to 4 p.m., in a room attached to the **Seamen's Institute, Hanover Street** (Entrance to Cookery Classes, Manesty Lane). The Lessons are by Demonstrations and Practice.

The Practical Class is limited to eight men at a time, who must be Cooks, Stewards, or Assistant Cooks.

Tickets of Admission to the Classes may be obtained on application to the Teacher, price 3/- payable in advance, for each Course of 12 Practice Lessons with accompanying Demonstrations.

Second and Third Courses of 12 Lessons can be arranged for.

The Committee are prepared to give a Certificate of Attendance to those who have attended either or both of these Courses.

As the Liverpool Shipowners' Association is actively interested in this movement, it is probable that holders of these Certificates will obtain a decided preference from Shipowners when seeking employment.

SCHOOL OF COOKERY,
    26, COLQUITT STREET, LIVERPOOL.

PREFACE.

SOME four years ago the then novel scheme of providing Cookery Classes for Seamen, with the view of improving the fare on board trading steamers and ships, was started by the Committee of the Liverpool Training School of Cookery. The scheme has proved very successful, evidently meeting a real need, and many Seamen have gained Certificates after a first, or second, and even a third course of lessons. Requests have constantly been made by these men, even from distant parts of the world, for a supply of recipes, a book form being preferred. To meet this demand, which grows louder day by day, the Committee of the Liverpool Training School of Cookery have authorised the publication of this manual, which contains recipes taught in the Seamen's Classes, and selected as being suitable to all the possibilities of sea life, with instructions as to modes of working. The Committee trust it will be found to supply the want so constantly expressed by those who have learned the value of systematic methods during the instruction they have availed themselves of in the Seamen's Cookery Classes.

FANNY L. CALDER,
Hon. Sec., Liverpool Training School of Cookery.

June, 1894.

INTRODUCTION.

ALTHOUGH there are literally Cookery books for the million, few of these are helpful to a Seaman, and it is hoped the following instructions and recipes, prepared specially for Sea Cooks, by a Sea Cook, may supply a want which has been more keenly felt than expressed. They are the outcome of 21 years of practical experience at sea, and of two years' endeavour on shore to give the benefits of that experience to others.

The work of a Cook at sea is, in most ways, much more difficult than that of one on shore. Where there is no market, its place must be taken to a very large extent by forethought, and this, not only in the providing—which is not always in the Cook's hands, but in the careful stowing and storing of his goods.

In these days of canning and compressing, the complaint of want of space may be set aside. A very small corner will give sufficient room for the storage of herbs and seasonings, without which much food is tasteless, and with which all may be improved. The careful packing away and arranging of the supply of fresh meat and vegetables with which one always starts even the longest voyage, may considerably delay the evil day when one must begin to depend on preserved food.

This matter, however, must be attended to beforehand. To leave it till the ship is at sea, and the day is only long enough for the day's work, is to prove oneself unfit for one's post, and to rob both master and men.

A good Cook will endeavour to suit the food, both in selection and preparation, to the climate, and for this a knowledge of the action and purpose of food is needed.

Food may be divided into three main sections. I., Flesh-forming. II., Heat-giving. III., Bone-making. Flesh-forming foods consist very largely of flesh, though many other materials belong to this section. Heat-giving foods may be again divided into two classes. (1) Fat. (2) Starch. The bone-making are principally fruits and vegetables, with salt, and the mineral matters found in all foods. It may soon be decided which of these classes must be placed first in order of value, according to the changes of climate to which a seaman is subjected, and an intelligent cook will endeavour, with the materials at his command, to follow the necessity of the case in providing meals. The method of cooking, also, largely affects the value of the food, under different circumstances.

It follows, therefore, that considerably more than a practical knowledge of the way to cook certain materials is essential to good Cookery, and it is hoped that the instructions given here may be helpful to those who desire intelligently and conscientiously to carry out the duties of the posts they occupy.

METHODS OF COOKERY.

There are six chief methods of Cookery—Roasting, Baking, Boiling, Stewing, Frying, and Broiling.

1. ROASTING is cooking by the direct rays of heat from a clear open fire and in a current of air.

RULES FOR ROASTING.—RED MEATS, *i.e.*, Beef or Mutton. Allow 15 minutes to the lb., and 15 minutes over for thin pieces, 20 minutes to the lb., and 20 minutes over for thick pieces.

WHITE MEATS, *i.e.*, Veal or Pork. Allow 20 minutes to the lb., and 20 minutes over for thin pieces, 25 minutes to the lb. for thick.

The fire must be built up some time before, and very hot and bright when the roasting begins. Put the joint quite close to the fire for the first 5 minutes. The extreme heat will harden the surface, and so keep in the juices of the meat. After 5 minutes draw back the joint that the meat may cook more slowly.

Keep the meat constantly turning, and baste frequently. Much of the success of roasting depends upon good basting.

BAKING is cooking in close dry heat, as in an oven, where the air is rarely changed.

Meats are frequently Baked, as this method is often more convenient than Roasting.

RULES FOR BAKING. 1. Allow the same length of time per lb. as for roasting.

2. Let the oven be at the first hot enough to harden the surface of the meat. Afterwards reduce the heat.

3. The meat must be well basted, and if one part of the oven is much hotter than another the joint may require to be turned occasionally.

Ovens are sometimes heated from above, sometimes from below. Either "top heat" or "bottom heat" will bake meat successfully, but bread, cakes, or any mixtures that should rise much in the cooking, require heat from below. Top heat hardens the upper surface of such things before they have risen.

RULES FOR BAKING PASTRY, BREAD, AND CAKES.—Pastry requires a hot oven. For bread the oven must be hot at first, then gradually reduce the heat and finish at a comparatively low temperature. The baking of cakes depends partly upon the ingredients used, but all large cakes require long baking and only moderate heat.

BOILING is cooking in sufficient water to cover the material.

RULES FOR BOILING MEAT.—1. Allow the same length of time as for roasting.

2. When boiling *fresh* meat, plunge it into fast boiling water sufficient to cover it; let the water again come to the boil, and boil for five minutes, this hardens the outside and keeps in the juices. After this keep the water much below boiling point, simmering gently for the rest of the time.

When boiling *salt* meat, put it into lukewarm, or if very salt, into cold water, to draw out some of the salt, bring to the boil and finish in the same way as fresh meat.

3. Remove all scum that rises. If not removed it may settle on the meat and discolour it.

RULES FOR BOILING VEGETABLES.—With the exception of old potatoes, peas, and spinach, vegetables should be put into boiling salted water, which must be kept boiling till the vegetables are cooked.

Old potatoes should be put into cold water. Like other root vegetables they should boil slowly with the lid on the pan.

Peas are put into hot, but not boiling water.

Spinach is boiled in its own juice.

Green vegetables should be boiled quickly with the lid off the pan. A little soda or sugar may be added to help to preserve the colour.

STEWING is cooking with a small quantity of liquid in a closely covered vessel. Very coarse pieces of meat may be made tender by long and careful stewing.

RULES FOR STEWING.—1. The heat should never rise above simmering point.

2. The length of time varies with the quality of the meat; very gentle stewing should go on until the meat is tender.

3. Keep the stewpan covered with a closely fitting lid.

FRYING is cooking in hot fat. This may be done in a shallow frying pan with a small quantity of fat, when it is called " dry frying "; or in a pan deep enough to hold fat to cover the article to be fried. The latter is called " wet frying," and the pan of fat is called the " bath."

RULES FOR FRYING.—-1. Before putting in the meat the fat must be very hot. The right heat can be told by carefully watching the fat. As long as it bubbles like boiling water it is too cold. When it becomes quite still and a pale blue vapour is seen rising from the surface, the fat is sufficiently hot. If heated till a brown smoke appears, the fat will be burnt and spoiled.

2. Articles must be made perfectly dry before frying.

3. Before serving fried foods free them from grease on clean soft paper.

4. Fat kept for frying purposes should be cooled and carefully strained after each time of using. If this is done it will keep good for a great length of time, and may be used again and again.

BROILING OR GRILLING is cooking on a gridiron, or a very hot frying pan, over a clear hot fire. It is suitable for small things, as steaks, chops, fish, &c.

RULES FOR BROILING.—1. The gridiron should be hot and well greased before using.

2. A hot smokeless fire is essential.

3. Hold the meat quite close to the fire until the outside is hardened so as to keep in the juice, then raise the gridiron a little.

4. Turn frequently or the juices will escape on the side furthest from the fire. Do not prick lean meat when turning, but keep the surface unbroken.

STEAMING is a modification of boiling, and is generally applied to Puddings. These are placed in basins or moulds covered with paper, and set in boiling water deep enough to come half-way up the mould. Longer time must be allowed for steaming than for boiling, the water must not be allowed to waste, and must be kept boiling all the time.

Invalids' food and small articles are also steamed by being placed between two plates set over boiling water.

THE CARE OF LIVE STOCK.

As a rule it is difficult to keep live stock in good condition when on board ship, for not only is it impossible to give the animals such lodging, exercise, and food as they would have on land, but stormy weather does great damage to live stock.

POULTRY.

Besides Indian corn and other dry food, poultry should have some moist food given to them. Soup left from the crew's table, if unfit for serving again, may be thickened with meal and given to poultry. Meal and water is also good for them, and almost all refuse from the table may be used for this purpose.

Provide whitewashed coops for poultry, with plenty of good, dry ashes under foot.

SHEEP

must be kept as dry as possible, and well fed regularly, and with a variety of food. Different kinds of grain should be given, also meal, bran, dry sweet hay, and clean water. A little salt in the food is necessary at least once a week.

PIGS

should be kept as clean as possible, and fed regularly. Moist foods are best in hot weather. In cold weather the food should be warm, but not hot. Too hot food causes disease and makes the pork unfit for use.

Boiled potato peelings, cold porridge, cabbage leaves, soups, and any kind of refuse from the table may be given to pigs. A little small coal should be given once or twice a week.

In very cold weather pigs should be kept warm by covering up their house, and giving them a bed of straw or shavings.

CATTLE

very rarely fatten on board ship, but with good care and regular feeding they need not lose much weight.

Good clean water, dry hay, a few slices of Swede turnips, a couple of clean carrots, and now and then a little corn, to help to improve the appetite of a beast after a few days on board. Their water *must* be clean and fresh.

THE KILLING AND DRESSING OF LIVE STOCK.

In the dressing of Cattle, Sheep, and Pigs, great care must be taken not to cut the gall bags, as this will spoil the meat.

As soon as a beast is cut down hang it in a place sheltered from rain or spray, which always tend to make the meat go bad.

TO KILL AND DRESS A PIG.

First tie up his mouth with a stout rope yarn to smother his cries, and fasten a hand line to one of his hind legs. Let him out of his house, keeping hold of the hand line, and lead him to a clean part of the scuppers, then turn him on his side and fasten his other three feet together with a stout rope yarn.

Open the neck with a sharp knife on the left side of the windpipe, sever the jugular veins, and work out the blood as quickly as possible. When quite dead and thoroughly bled wash away the blood, pour over the pig boiling water with a little cold water added, and scrape thoroughly clean all over.

Hang the beast up to the rigging by the gambel, wash it well, and then wipe it quite dry. Cut the pig open and remove the offal, wash the inside well with a piece of linen or muslin, open nicely with the pricker, and leave all night covered with a meat sheet.

TO CUT UP A PIG.

Split the breast open to the neck, cut off the head, open the whole front of the pig from neck to tail. Split down the centre of the back and cut each of the two sides into the following six joints:—

Joints.	Method of Cooking.
1 Spare Rib	Roasted
2 Hand	Pickled or boiled
3 Spring or Belly	Salted and Dried for Bacon
4 Fore Loin	The THICK END for Chops / The THIN END for Roasting
5 Loin	Roasted or Cut into Chops
6 Leg	Roasted or Cured for Ham

The HEAD is usually split, salted and kept in pickle for 3 or 4 days. The FEET must be well cleaned and cooked as Pettitoes. The LIVER and SWEETBREAD are cooked as Pig's-fry.

N.B.—All spare fat must be boiled down for lard.

TO KILL A SHEEP.

Tie together the fore and one of the hind feet, place the sheep on its left side near the scupper, and press the body with the knee. Hold the head with the left hand and with the right pass the knife quickly through the neck—between the windpipe and the bones of the neck—near the angle of the jaw. This severs the jugular vein. Now break the neck by placing the right hand on the nape and giving the head a sharp jerk backwards with the left hand.

The sheep is then left about 10 minutes before dressing.

TO DRESS A SHEEP.

Remove the fastenings from the feet. Lay the sheep on its back, lift a little of the skin just above the fore foot with the left hand, and cut it off. Insert the knife under the skin at the inside of the fore foot, and run the knife to the beginning of the breast. Remove the skin quickly from the shoulder to the foot. Treat the other shoulder in the same manner, taking care to run the knife to the same point above the breast. Draw the skin from the breast and proceed to skin the legs. Remove the skin in the same way as when doing the shoulders, but keep the cuts straight across where the skin has least wool. When the legs, shoulders, and breast are finished, run the knife straight up the belly to the breast, cut off the feet below the knees and hocks, draw out the gullet, tie in a knot, place the gambel in the hamstrings, and draw the sheep up to the rigging. Draw out the tail and remove the skin from the sides, drawing it down from the back to the neck. Cut off the head. Wipe the sheep down with a clean wet cloth. Cut away the offal, saw the breast through, remove the pluck and throw away the obnoxious parts. String up the shoulders with a short noose. Wipe out the carcase, trim the neck, and cover the sheep, leaving it in a clean cool place.

In ordinary weather sheep should be killed 24 hours before being cut up.

In hot weather kill at sunset and cut up the meat next morning.

TO KEEP SKINS.

Dry them well in the sun and keep in a dry place afterwards. Or sprinkle plenty of salt on the inside and roll up with the outer edges turned in. Tie up in a tight parcel. These will keep for six months.

TO CUT UP A SHEEP.

Split down the centre of the back or chine. Cut in halves, and each half into six joints.

Joints.	Method of Cooking.
1 Leg	Roasted or Boiled
2 Loin	Chops or Roasted
3 Best End of Neck	Cutlets
4 Shoulder	Roasted or Baked
5 Scrag End of Neck	For Chops or Pies
6 Breast	Roasted or Stewed

N.B.—A Saddle of Mutton is composed of the two loins undivided. A Haunch of Mutton is the leg and loin in one piece.

TO KILL A BULLOCK.

Tie a stout line to the animal's neck, and lead him to a ring-bolt on the deck. Pass the line through the bolt and bring his nose to the deck. This being done, take the pole or carpenter's maul, and drop the beast with all speed. Open the neck. Cut through the jugular vein. Work the blood out till the beast is quite dead. Remove the skin from the head. Chop off the horns. Turn the beast over on his back.

Pritch him up and skin the brisket. Joint the knees and hocks as in a sheep. Remove the skin from the hind quarter.

Remove the useless parts near the tail. Divide the cod fat evenly, and cut the belly through to the aitch bone.

Remove the caul. Saw the brisket through. Divide the aitch bone.

Run a stout capstan bar through the ham strings and fasten it with clean rope yarn to prevent the bar slipping. Hoist up to the rigging stay.

Skin the tail. Remove the offal, leaving the kidneys intact. Take off the hide. Wipe the beast down with lukewarm water and a clean cloth.

Open the brisket. Remove the gullet, windpipe, heart, and lights. Wipe down the inside of the breast.

Saw through the sacrum, and chop through the back bone. Cut through the spinal bones with a knife, leaving the alternate ones on each side of the beef. Trim out the veins of the shoulders and trim and wipe the neck. Cover in a dry cool place. Cut up for use after 24 hours.

TO CUT UP A BULLOCK.

After the beast has been cut in two and then quartered, it is divided into the following joints :—

Joints.	Method of Cooking.
1 Sirloin	Roasted
2 Rump	Used for Steaks, &c.
3 Aitchbone	Roasted or Boiled
4 Buttock	Stewed
5 Mouse Round	Stewed
6 Veiny Piece	Stewed
7 Thick Flank	Stewed, or Rolled and Boiled
8 Thin Flank	Stewed
9 Leg	Stewed (as Steak)
10 Fore Rib	Roasted
11 Middle Rib	Roasted
12 Chuck Rib	Stewed
13 Leg of Mutton Piece	Stewed, used for Pies, &c.
14 Brisket	Stewed
15 Clod	Stewed or Corned
16 Neck	Stewed
17 Shin	Stewed
18 Cheek	Stewed for various made dishes.

CORNED BEEF.

Those parts of the animal which are to be Corned must be put into pickle as soon as the beast is cut up.

Should the meat be left until there is the slightest sourness or decay, it will never be made sweet in the corning process.

TO CORN BEEF.

Cut the joints to the size required. Prick the outer skin with the point of a sharp knife. Mix together ½ lb. saltpetre and 20 lbs. rough salt. Rub the meat well with this.

Put a layer of meat at the bottom of the draining tub, and cover it with plenty of salt. Repeat this until the meat is finished.

Leave the meat for 12 hours, then take it out and again cover it with fresh salt, putting plenty of salt on the top of each layer as in the first instance.

Leave it to drain 24 hours.

Take out the meat, and place in a good strong pickle made of the following ingredients :—

PICKLE FOR ONE CWT. OF BEEF.

4 gallons of fresh water.	1 quart of lime juice.
3 pounds of brown sugar.	4 oz. saltpetre.

As much salt as will allow a potato to float in the brine.

METHOD.—Put the water in harness casks, and throw in a good sized potato. Keep adding salt and stir well till the potato swims on the surface.

Add the lime juice, sugar, and saltpetre.

Stir for ten minutes.

Take out the potato and put the meat in the pickle.

This will keep in a shady place for six or eight months.

N.B.—Take care to keep the sun from the casks.

A good draining tub may be made out of a pork cask by boring half a dozen auger holes in the bottom. Lay in it two or three blocks of wood, on edge, and over these lay pieces of wood to make a platform for the meat, so that it can drain without lying in the liquid. Should the meat lie all night in the liquid that runs from it the chances are that in warm weather it will all go bad, and nothing will make meat eatable after it is once tainted.

TO CURE HAMS.

When the pig is fit to be cut up take off the hams and rub them well with common salt. Lay them at the bottom of the draining-tub. Cover them with plenty of salt, and let them remain for two or three days in a cool place.

PICKLE FOR TWO HAMS, 14 to 16 lbs. Weight

Mix together

> 1 quart of vinegar.
> 2 ozs. of saltpetre.
> 1½ lbs. of salt.
> 1 lb. of sugar.

Place the hams in a vessel just large enough to hold them. Pour over the pickle, and turn them in the pickle every day for about 25 days. At the end of this time hang them up to dry for four days. Cover the fleshy side of the hams thickly with pea-meal. The hams will be ready for use after another week, or they may be kept for the latter part of the voyage when most stores are coming to an end.

TO KILL AND PREPARE POULTRY, &c.

In choosing poultry for the table it is important to remember the manner in which it is to be cooked. Old fowls should not be chosen for either roasting or boiling; they need long and slow cooking and are suitable only for ragoûts, stew, or curries. If an old fowl must be roasted it is an improvement to first partly cook it in the stock-pot, and afterwards finish the cooking by roasting.

Birds casting their feathers should not be chosen for the table.

RABBITS AND HARES.—The best way of killing is to give a sharp knock at the top of the head with a stout piece of wood. If properly done one knock will cause instant death.

BIRDS.—Before killing birds fasten the wings together. Turkeys, geese, and ducks should be killed by severing the jugular veins. Fowls and pigeons are killed by breaking the neck close to the head: this is done by a sharp pull of the head, while the body is held firmly.

Before plucking birds they may scalded, to make the process of plucking easier. Plunge them into hot but not boiling water for about half a minute. When one of the wing feathers will come away with a moderate pull the bird is sufficiently scalded. If left too long in the hot water the skin becomes soft and breaks away when the feathers are plucked, thus spoiling the appearance of the bird. After plucking singe to remove any down or small feathers.

TO TRUSS POULTRY.

Rabbit for Boiling.—Empty, skin and wash the rabbit, take out the eyes; if liked, put in the stuffing and sew up. Cut off the fore joints of the shoulders and legs, draw them up to the sides of the body and skewer firmly. Bring the head round and skewer it to the side.

Hare for Roasting.—Truss in the same way as rabbit, but leave on the ears, and instead of bringing the head to the side of the body, raise it, and skewer firmly between the shoulders.

Turkey.—Draw the sinews from the legs by means of a hook. Turn the turkey breast downwards. Cut a slit in the back of the neck. Loosen the skin. Cut off the neck close to the body leaving a piece of skin fully two inches long for folding over the back. Take out the crop. Loosen the liver and the rest of the inside at the throat end. Then cut a small hole at the vent, and draw the bird, being careful not to break the gall-bag. Flatten the breast bone. Cut off the feet, scald the legs, and peel off the outer skin. Lay the turkey flat on the back. Skewer the legs and wings to the side, pressing them downwards so as to make the bird stand firm for the convenience of the carver. Put in the stuffing at the neck, and turn back the flap of skin to keep the stuffing in its place.

Goose.—Cut off the feet and the first joint of the pinions. Cut off the neck and draw in the same way as turkey. Skewer the wings and legs to the sides of the body. Fasten back the skin at the neck, and after stuffing, close up the other end of the bird by making a slit in the skin of the body and passing the tail through it.

Ducks.—Truss in the same way as geese, but leave on the feet, and turn them back upon the body, so as to keep the legs in position without the use of a skewer.

Fowls and Pigeons.—When trussing fowls and pigeons for roasting, after drawing the bird cut off the toes at the first joint. Scald the feet and legs and remove the outer skin. Cut off the neck, leaving a piece of skin to turn over the back. Twist the pinions that their points are brought across the back of the bird. Press the legs firmly to the sides of the body, and fasten them with a skewer run through the upper part of the thighs. Tie the feet together, then tie them to the tail. Fowls for boiling are trussed in almost the same way, but for boiling cut off the legs at the first joint, loosen the skin round the legs till they can be pushed back inside the body, then close up neatly by making a slit in the skin and passing the tail through it.

TO PRESERVE EGGS.

Eggs may be preserved for four or five months by the following methods.

Melt some mutton suet, and when it is beginning to solidify cover the eggs with it. The eggs may be left in the fat, or may simply be coated with fat and kept in a cool store room. Another effectual plan is to give the eggs a good coating of glue, thick gum, or varnish.

All these methods, by preventing the passage of air into the eggs, will keep good eggs in a sound condition for several months.

LIST OF STORE SEASONINGS SUFFICIENT FOR

TWELVE MONTHS' VOYAGE.

12 bunches of marjoram.
18 ,, ,, thyme.
18 ,, ,, sage.
12 ,, ,, mint.
24 ,, ,, parsley.
2 lbs. of cloves.
1 lb. ,, mixed spice.
1 lb. ,, bayleaves.

N.B.—As the supply of these articles is somewhat limited, it is recommended that the cook brings the stock up to the above list before sailing.

SAUCES.
(Savoury).

MELTED BUTTER.

INGREDIENTS.

1 tablespoonful butter.	½ pint water,
1 tablespoonful flour.	Pinch of salt.

METHOD.—Melt the butter slightly, add the flour. Mix quite smooth. Add the water gradually stirring all the time to prevent lumps. Boil 3 minutes. Add salt, &c., and serve.

This sauce is the foundation of many others, and may be varied indefinitely. With the addition of anchovy essence it becomes anchovy sauce, suitable for serving with fish. The addition of chopped parsley makes it into parsley sauce, &c., &c.

SORREL SAUCE.

Wash and pick some sorrel, put it into a stew pan with the water that clings to it. Keep stirring to prevent burning. When cooked lay it on a sieve to drain. Chop it finely and stew it with 4 tablespoonsful of gravy and a small piece of butter. Rub through a wire sieve. If too acid a little sugar may be added.

As a subsitute for sorrel use a good London lettuce in the same way, adding a little vinegar to the lettuce sauce.

PARSLEY SAUCE.

INGREDIENTS.

1 tablespoonful butter.	¼ pint milk.
1 tablespoonful flour.	¼ pint water.
1 tablespoonful finely chopped parsley.	Salt and pepper.

Put the butter into a saucepan, and allow it to melt. Then mix in the flour smoothly. Add by degrees the water, stirring well all the time, then the milk, and boil 3 minutes. Add the salt and pepper, and the parsley last thing before serving.

If this sauce is to be used for fish, ¼ pint of fish stock may be used instead of water.

EGG SAUCE (FOR FISH).

INGREDIENTS.

1 tablespoonful butter.	¼ pint milk.
1 tablespoonful flour.	¼ pint water,
2 hardboiled eggs.	or fish stock.

METHOD.—Melt the butter in a saucepan, add the flour. Mix quite smooth over a gentle heat. Add gradually the liquids, and boil 3 minutes. Stir in the finely chopped eggs and serve.

BREAD SAUCE.

INGREDIENTS.

½ pint of milk.	2 ozs. stale bread crumbs.
1 onion.	3 cloves.
6 peppercorns.	½ teaspoonful salt.
½ oz. of butter.	

Put the milk, onion, cloves, and peppercorns in a saucepan, cover it and set it by the *side* of the fire for 10 to 20 minutes. (10 minutes will lightly extract the onion flavour, 20 minutes will make it stronger). Strain the milk, and put back in the saucepan ; if the milk is wasted, enough must be added to make up the ½ pint, then add the crumbs and set it over a gentle heat for 15 minutes, stirring with a wooden spoon ; it should simmer, but care must be taken not to let it burn ; add salt, and if liked, a pinch of cayenne. Stir in the butter and boil up once.

APPLE SAUCE.

INGREDIENTS.

1 bottle of preserved apples,	¼ pt. water.
or six fresh apples.	A little sugar.

METHOD.—The apples being free from skin and core, must be cut up and placed in a pan with the water. Simmer till the apples are soft. Beat up to a pulp, and sweeten to taste.

HORSERADISH SAUCE.

INGREDIENTS.

4 tablespoonsful grated horseradish.	½ teaspoonful pepper.
1 teaspoonful sugar.	1 teaspoonful mixed mustard.
1 teaspoonful salt.	Vinegar.

METHOD.—Mix together the horseradish, sugar, salt, pepper, and mustard. Moisten with sufficient vinegar to give the sauce the consistency of thick cream. Serve hot or cold.

To heat this sauce put it in a jar and set in boiling water. Do not boil the sauce, or it will curdle.

ITALIAN SAUCE.

INGREDIENTS.

2 pickled walnuts.	Juice of half a lemon.
4 shallots or young onions.	1 teaspoonful chopped parsley.
1 head of garlic.	½ teaspoonful sugar.
½ pt. stock.	Salt and pepper.
½ glass sherry.	

METHOD.—Chop the walnuts and shallots. Put all ingredients except the sherry into a closely covered saucepan, and simmer twenty minutes. Strain, add the sherry, reheat and serve.

MINT SAUCE.

INGREDIENTS.

2 tablespoonsful chopped mint.
1 tablespoonful sugar.
¼ pint malt vinegar.

METHOD.—Have the mint clean and dry. Pick the leaves from the stalk and chop them finely. Add the chopped leaves to the vinegar and sugar. This sauce should be made two or three hours before it is to be used, so that the vinegar may be well flavoured by the mint.

Dry mint may be used when fresh cannot be obtained.

BLONDE SAUCE.

INGREDIENTS.

½ pint melted butter (sauce). | 1 dessertspoonful chopped
¼ pint stock. | parsley.
1 onion finely chopped. | 1 glass sherry.
1 lemon. | 3 yolks.

METHOD.—Put the stock and melted butter into a saucepan, add the chopped onion and parsley, the lemon rind, and the juice of the lemon. Simmer slowly for 20 minutes. Add the beaten yolks, and the sherry, and strain through a sieve. Season and serve.

MAYONNAISE SAUCE.

INGREDIENTS.

1 raw yolk of egg. | Very little cayenne.
1 saltspoonful mustard. | Salad oil.
Salt and pepper. |

METHOD.—Mix together the yolk, pepper, salt and cayenne. Add salad oil carefully drop by drop stirring all the time, till the sauce becomes as thick as butter. A teaspoonful of malt vinegar may be stirred in at the last.

SAUCES.
(*Sweet.*)

WHITE SAUCE.

INGREDIENTS.

1 tablespoonful butter. | ½ pint milk.
1 tablespoonful flour. | A few drops vanilla essence.
1 tablespoonful sugar. |

METHOD.— Melt the butter in a sauce pan, add the flour and mix smooth. Add the milk, by degrees, stirring all the time. Boil 3 minutes. Stir in the sugar and flavouring and serve.

SHERRY SAUCE.

INGREDIENTS.

½ pint melted butter (sauce.) | 1 glass sherry.
1 tablespoonful sugar. | 2 or 3 drops cochineal.

METHOD.—Add the sugar and sherry to the melted butter. Colour with cochineal. Bring the whole to boiling point and serve.

PORT WINE SAUCE.

INGREDIENTS.

½ pint melted butter (sauce.) | 1 tablespoonful sugar.
1 glass port wine. | 1 tablespoonful lemon juice.

METHOD.—Add to the melted butter all the other ingredients. Simmer together for five minutes and serve.

LEMON SAUCE.

INGREDIENTS.

1 tablespoonful butter. | 1 tablespoonful sugar.
1 tablespoonful flour. | Rind and juice of 1 lemon.
½ pint milk. | Pinch of salt.

METHOD.—Melt the butter in a saucepan, add the flour, and mix smooth. Add by degrees the milk, stirring all the time, then the grated lemon rind, the sugar and the salt. Boil 3 minutes. The strained lemon juice must be added just before serving.

CRANBERRY SAUCE.

INGREDIENTS.

1 tablespoonful butter. | ¼ pint water.
1 dessertspoonful arrowroot. | ½ pint cranberries.
2 tablespoonsful sugar. |

METHOD.—Put the cranberries, butter and water into a saucepan. Cover the pan and simmer for 20 minutes, or till the cranberries are soft. Add the sugar. Put the fruit through a sieve, and return it to the pan. Moisten the arrowroot with a little water, add it to the cranberries, and boil the whole for 3 minutes.

COLOURED SYRUP (FOR PUDDINGS).

INGREDIENTS.

¼ lb. white sugar.	3 or 4 drops cochineal.
½ pint water.	A few drops essence of lemon.

METHOD.—Put the sugar, water, and cochineal in a pan. Boil till the liquid becomes clear, thick and syrupy. Add the flavouring essence and serve.

JAM SAUCE.

INGREDIENTS.

1 tablespoonful butter.	¼ lb. black currant jelly or
1 tablespoonful corn flour.	jam.
½ pint water.	1 tablespoonful sugar.

METHOD.—Put the water with the jelly or jam into a saucepan, add the sugar, boil and strain. Put the butter into a clean pan, when partly melted add the flour, and mix quite smooth. Add by degrees the strained juice, stirring all the time. Boil three minutes and serve.

ARROWROOT SAUCE.

INGREDIENTS.

The juice of 1 bottle of fruit.	2 dessert spoonsful arrowroot.
4 ozs. sugar.	A few drops of cochineal.

METHOD.—Strain the juice, and colour it with the cochineal. Add the sugar, and boil for five minutes. Mix the arrowroot smoothly with a very little cold water, add it to the boiling syrup, and boil all together for three minutes, stirring all the time.

BRANDY SAUCE.

INGREDIENTS.

2 tablespoonfuls butter.	1 glass brandy.
1 tablespoonful flour.	½ pt. water.
1 tablespoonful sugar.	

METHOD.—Melt the butter in a saucepan, add the flour and mix smooth. Add the water by degrees, stirring all the time. Boil 3 minutes. Add the sugar and the brandy just before serving.

FIRST COURSE.

BROWN VEGETABLE SOUP.

INGREDIENTS.

4 quarts fresh stock.	4 tablespoonsful flour.
2 small carrots.	4 tablespoonsful dripping.
2 small onions.	⅓ teaspoonful pepper.
1 spring turnip.	Enough salt to taste.
½ bunch thyme.	A little parsley.
4 cloves.	

METHOD.—Put the dripping into a stewpan. Make it hot and brown one onion, remove it, brown the flour, and then add the stock. Stick the cloves into the sides of one whole onion, add the vegetables cut very small, herbs and pepper, and simmer slowly one hour. Remove the onion and cloves, add pepper and salt, and simmer another ten minutes. Skim off all fat before serving it, with a little chopped parsley put in the tureen.

PEA SOUP.

INGREDIENTS.

8 quarts water.	2 tablespoonsful dripping.
3 pints split peas.	4 lb. piece of half cooked salt
2 carrots, or piece of turnip same size.	pork, or sufficient salt stock to season.
2 tablespoonsful celery seed.	1 teaspoonful sugar.
2 ,, flour.	6 leaves of mint.

METHOD.—Make the dripping hot in a large stew pan, slightly brown the flour, add celery seed and water, and stir well until boiling, then add the peas, mint, sugar, and carrots, and simmer for two hours in covered pan. Add the pork, or stock, and simmer another half hour, rub all through a wire sieve and warm up again before serving. It is not advisable to steep peas all night in warm weather as the water becomes sour.

POTATO SOUP.
INGREDIENTS.

6 quarts water.	3 tablespoonsful flour.
5 lbs. potatoes.	6 ozs. or 6 tablespoonsful of sago.
2 tablespoonsful thick milk.	
1 ,, pepper.	8 cloves.
3 ,, dripping.	Salt stock to season.

METHOD. —Put the dripping into a large stew pan and make it hot. Then fry the flour a good brown, add the water, potatoes, peeled and cut into slices, cloves, milk, and stock, and simmer for one hour. Then add sago, and simmer again ten minutes. Strain all through a sieve, rubbing the potatoes through into the liquor. Re-heat and serve. Sufficient for twelve.

BEAN SOUP. SALT STOCK.
INGREDIENTS.

4 quarts water.	3 cloves.
1 pint cooked beans.	1 tablespoonful flour.
2 leaves of mint.	1 tablespoonful dripping.
2 bay leaves.	½ teaspoonful white pepper.
1 small garlic pod.	Salt stock to season.

METHOD.—Make the dripping hot in a stew pan, brown the flour slightly, add the stock, beans, and other ingredients, and simmer slowly for 1 hour. Strain through a wire sieve, rub beans through, skim off the fat, and reheat in the stew pan.

MULLIGATAWNY SOUP.
INGREDIENTS.

4 quarts fresh stock.	½ cold chicken.
4 tablespoonsful curry powder.	6 cloves.
4 tablespoonsful dripping.	A pinch of cayenne pepper, and salt to taste.
4 tablespoonsful flour.	
6 forcemeat balls.	2 small onions.

METHOD.—Make the dripping hot in a stew pan. Brown the onions sliced, take them out and brown the flour, then add the curry powder, cayenne, and half the stock, simmer slowly half-an-hour, then strain it off. Return it to a pan and add the remaining stock, the chicken cut small, and the forcemeat balls. Season and simmer another half-hour before serving. Boiled rice as for curry should accompany this soup, served separately.

BARLEY BROTH with SALT BEEF FOR STOCK.

INGREDIENTS.

6 quarts water.	½ teaspoonful black pepper.
1 tablespoonful dripping.	A pinch of pepper.
1 tablespoonful flour.	7 cloves.
½ lb. barley.	A 4 lb. piece salt beef half
3 oz. pressed vegetables, or	cooked.
1 carrot and ½ turnip.	

METHOD.—Make the dripping hot. Brown the flour a nice golden brown, then add the water gradually, keeping it well stirred. When boiling add the barley well washed, the vegetables steeped for 10 minutes, the cloves, cayenne, black pepper and beef. Leave the beef in until the soup is sufficiently salt; take care to remove all signs of fat by skimming, and by laying clean paper on the top of the soup; this will remove what grease the ladle leaves behind. Time to cook the barley, 2 hours.

SOUP AND DOUILLI

INGREDIENTS.

4 quarts fresh stock.	2 small onions.
4 tablespoonsful flour.	1 lb. shin beef.
4 tablespoonsful dripping.	A pinch of cayenne.
½ bunch marjoram.	Salt to taste.
1 small carrot.	

METHOD.—Make the dripping hot in a stew pan. Brown the beef cut small, take it out, brown the onions cut small, take these out, and brown the flour a good colour, add the stock gradually, keeping it well stirred. When simmering add the marjoram tied in a piece of muslin, and leave it in 10 minutes, then add the carrot cut small, season and simmer 1 hour. Before serving remove all fat.

LING AND EGG SAUCE.

Remove the outer skin of the fish, taking care to leave the under skin to hold the flakes of the fish together. Cut it into two inch squares. Steep well in plenty of salt water, then place in a fish-kettle of boiling water, and simmer slowly three-quarters of an hour. Take the fish out of the boiler by lifting the strainer, and dish it up without breaking the squares.

EGG SAUCE.

1 hard boiled egg.	2 tablespoonfuls flour.
1 tablespoonful butter.	$\frac{1}{4}$ pint milk and $\frac{1}{2}$ pint water.

Make the butter hot in a saucepan, add the flour, but do not brown it, add the milk gradually, stirring well, lastly add the water and a pinch of salt, and simmer for 10 minutes. Boil the egg for 20 minutes, remove the shell and chop it finely, add it to the sauce, and pour it over the fish. Garnish with sprigs of parsley if possible.

COLD FISH HASH.

INGREDIENTS.

2 lbs. cold fish.	3 gills of water.
2 small onions.	1 tablespoonful anchovy essence
2 lbs. raw potatoes.	1 tablespoonful dripping.
$\frac{1}{4}$ teaspoonful pepper.	1 tablespoonful flour.
A little chopped parsley.	Salt to taste.

METHOD.—Wash, peel, and slice the potatoes and cut them into halves. Bone the fish, and break it into flakes, slice the onions. Make the dripping hot in a stew pan. Brown the onions slightly, take them out, brown the flour, then add water. When boiled add half the potatoes and the fish, pepper, salt, anchovy ; add the remainder of the potatoes, cover and simmer 30 minutes. Sprinkle chopped parsley over all for the last five minutes.

CURRIED SALT BEEF.

(*Cold Meat Cookery.*)

INGREDIENTS.

1 lb. cooked salt beef.	1 tablespoonful butter or
2 small potatoes.	dripping.
2 dessertspoonsful curry	1 good sized onion.
powder.	1 teaspoonful vinegar.
1 dessertspoonful flour.	1 pinch of sugar.
	$\frac{1}{2}$ pint of water.

METHOD.—Make the dripping or butter hot in a stew pan. Brown the onion cut small, add the curry powder and flour dry and mix till smooth, then add the water gradually and keep it well stirred. Have the meat and potato cut small. If the meat be too salt, scald it and make it fresh before adding it to the curry. Add the other ingredients and simmer slowly for 30 minutes.

STEAMED RICE FOR CURRY.

Wash 1 lb. of rice in sea water and strain it off. Place it in a stew pan with 1 quart of fresh water, boil slowly for 10 minutes and strain off the water. Put the rice back into the pan, cover it with a clean cloth folded together thickly, cover the pan, and steam slowly 1 hour on a cool part of the range. This saves a great deal of water, and the rice retains the best part of the starch which it loses when boiled.

TO BOIL RICE.

Let the water be plentiful and boiling, put in the rice, and boil moderately fast for 20 minutes if Indian rice, and 25 minutes if American. Pour the rice into a colander, wash well with plenty of boiling water without breaking the rice. Place the colander over boiling water, cover with a clean cloth and steam ½ hour.

DRY HASH.
(Cold Meat Cookery.)
INGREDIENTS.

2 lbs. potatoes.	A little pepper.
½ lb. cooked, fresh or salt beef, or pork.	½ teaspoonful dried herbs.
1 small onion.	A little salt, if needed.

METHOD.—Wash, peel and boil the potatoes, dry them well, add the meat, the onion chopped finely, pepper and herbs, mash all well together, mould and brown in oven. To be garnished with grilled bacon.

BOWLING HASH.
(Cold Meat Cookery.)
INGREDIENTS.

1 lb. beef or pork, salt or fresh.	A pinch of cayenne pepper.
1 lb. potatoes.	¼ teaspoonful pepper.
1 small onion.	1 teaspoonful dripping.
½ pint water.	1 teaspoonful flour.
2 cloves.	A little sweet herbs.

METHOD.—Cut the meat and potatoes into small squares the size of dice, and the onion the same. Make the dripping hot in a stewpan. Brown the onion, take it out, and brown the flour a rich brown, add the water gradually, making a smooth roux, then add the meat, potatoes, onions, herbs, and cayenne, simmer twenty-five minutes. Add the pepper the last five minutes. If made with salt meat make it fresh by scalding after cutting it small, before adding it to the roux. If made with fresh meat, a little salt must be added.

BISCUIT HASH.

(Cold Meat Cookery.)

INGREDIENTS.

6 lbs. broken biscuits, steeped.	1 cooked carrot.
2 lbs. cold salt beef or pork.	1 cooked turnip.
¼ lb. dripping.	1 teaspoonful pepper.
2 onions.	1 teaspoonful mixed spice.

METHOD. – Chop the meat, onions, and vegetables finely; squeeze the water well out of the biscuits, and rub them through a coarse wire sieve; add all the other ingredients, and mix thoroughly. Put it into a baking tin, and brown in a moderate oven until firm. Cut into squares and serve.

BEEF À LA MARINE.

INGREDIENTS.

1 lb. salt beef.	¼ teaspoonful pepper.
1 good sized carrot.	1 teaspoonful vinegar.
1 good sized turnip.	1 teaspoonful dripping.
1 small onion.	1 teaspoonful flour.
2 cloves.	½ pint of water.

METHOD.—Make the dripping hot in the stewpan, and brown the onion and flour in the fat, stir well, and add the water gradually, stirring all the time. Have ready the meat cut into thin fillets, and made fresh by scalding. Add the meat to the gravy, put the carrot and turnip cut into thin strips over the meat, season, and simmer 1 hour.

HOT POT. TOM BOWLING.

INGREDIENTS.

25 lbs. potatoes.	½ lb. dripping.
6 ,, beef or preserved mutton.	½ oz. pepper.
	2 ,, salt.
3 ,, onions.	2 quarts water.

METHOD.—Wash, peel and cut the potatoes into small thick lumps. Place half in the bottom of a deep baking tin. Cut the meat the same size, lay it over the potatoes, then the onions minced, and the seasoning. Make the dripping warm in a stew pan and toss the remainder of the potatoes in it; put these on the top of meat, add the water and bake for 1½ to 2 hours. Sufficient for fifteen persons.

IRISH STEW.

INGREDIENTS.

5 lbs. potatoes.	½ small Swede turnip cut
1 lb. salt beef made fresh,	small.
and cut small.	2 small onions.
2 carrots.	Pepper, Water.

METHOD.—Wash and peel the potatoes and cut them in pieces. Put the meat on the top of the potatoes, add the carrots and turnips cut in pieces. Chop the onions, sprinkle them over all, add water sufficient to barely cover, season, and simmer slowly for 1½ hours without stirring. Irish stew must not be mixed until everything is well cooked and ready to serve.

HODGE PODGE.

INGREDIENTS.

1 lb. fresh beef.	1 bay leaf.
1 small carrot.	A little cayenne pepper.
1 small onion.	½ teaspoonful salt.
3 tablespoons cooked green peas.	1 teaspoonful flour.
A piece of garlic, size of a bean.	1 teaspoonful dripping.
	½ pint of water.

METHOD.—Cut the meat, carrot and onion into small dice shapes. Brown the onion and meat slightly in the hot fat. Then brown the flour, add the water and stir till smooth. Add the garlic cut finely, the bay leaf and cayenne, and simmer 10 minutes in the roux, and then strain. Return the gravy to the pan, add the meat, carrot, onions and peas, and simmer for 40 minutes before serving.

PORK AND BEANS.

INGREDIENTS.

4 lb. piece of fat pork.	1 dessertspoonful molasses.
1 lb. of beans.	¼ teaspoonful pepper.

METHOD.—Steep the pork if salt, simmer it slowly for 20 minutes in 2 quarts of water. Then throw away half the water and add the beans after steeping them for 4 hours, add more water and place in an earthenware jar, the rind of the pork being first removed. Cover the jar and place in a good oven. Bake 2 hours or until all the beans are tender, add the molasses and pepper the last ½ hour. Turn out on to a dish, cover the ends of the pork with beans, and brown in a quick oven.

MUTTON PUDDING. PRESERVED MUTTON.

INGREDIENTS.

1½ lbs. mutton.	½ lb. flour.
1 small onion.	3 ozs. suet.
½ teaspoonful pepper.	A little cold water.
¼ pint of water.	Salt as required.

METHOD.—Chop the suet finely, mix it with the flour, a pinch of salt if the suet is fresh, add enough cold water to make a nice firm dough. Grease a pudding mould and line it with the pastry. Cut the mutton into pieces the size of a chestnut, lay it in the mould, sprinkle with flour, salt, pepper, and onion chopped. Half fill the mould with water and cover with pastry. Cover the mould and steam for two hours.

PRESERVED MUTTON PIE.

INGREDIENTS.

2-lb. tin of preserved mutton.	1 tablespoonful dripping.
2 small onions.	Salt and pepper to season.
1 tablespoonful flour.	Little water.

METHOD.—Open the tin on the outer edge, and turn the meat on to a chopping board. Cut through twice, and place it in a pie dish. Make the dripping hot in a stew pan, brown the flour and onion, and add sufficient water to make a smooth gravy, and season with pepper and salt; pour it over the meat in the pie dish, then cover it with a suet puff paste, and bake in a quick oven half-an-hour.

TO BOIL OLD POTATOES.

If the potatoes are large and small cut the large ones, and have all as nearly as possible the same size. Put them on in cold water, over a brisk fire, add the salt to the water when boiling, and let them simmer rather quickly. In trying potatoes with a fork, select the largest, and if this is cooked, the smallest is bound to be so. Drain the water off thoroughly, return them to the range to dry a few seconds, taking care not to shake the potatoes in the water after they are cooked.

Shake the bottom potatoes to the top, and cover with a clean cloth until sent to table.

PEAS PUDDING.

INGREDIENTS.

1 lb. split peas.	3 leaves of mint.
2 ozs. raw salt pork.	¼ teaspoonful pepper.

METHOD.—Tie all the ingredients in a clean cloth, and simmer slowly 2 hours in plenty of water. Rub through a sieve and brown in oven. Always served with salt pork or boiled bacon.

PLAIN SUET PUDDING.

INGREDIENTS.

6 ozs. flour.	⅛ teaspoonful baking powder.
6 ,, bread.	½ ,, salt.
3 ,, suet.	¼ pint cold water.

METHOD. Chop the suet finely, removing all skin and fibre. Steep the bread in cold water, then squeeze it well through a clean cloth, and add it to the flour and suet. Mix well together, adding baking powder and salt. Mix all to a smooth dough with water. Put into a well greased mould and steam 2 hours.

RICE PUDDING (WITHOUT EGGS).

INGREDIENTS.

3 gills of water.	2 dessertspoonsful sugar.
2 tablespoonsful condensed milk.	1 teaspoonful butter.
2½ tablespoonsful rice.	Dust of mixed spice.

METHOD.— Mix two tablespoonsful of condensed milk with the water and sugar. Pour it into a pie dish, add the rice well washed and the butter. The spice is to float on the top, not to be stirred up with the milk. Place the pudding at the bottom of the oven until well baked. In bad weather boil the rice with the milk and sugar until well cooked; then place it in the oven to brown with the butter and spice on the top.

TREACLE PUDDING.

INGREDIENTS :—

1½ lbs. steeped bread, or crew's small biscuits.	½ teaspoonful powdered ginger.
	1 ,, baking powder.
1 large tablespoonful molasses.	2 tablespoonsful sugar.
1 ,, ,, lime juice.	2 ozs. suet.

METHOD.—Squeeze the water well out of the bread, put it into a mixing bowl, add molasses, ginger, suet—chopped very fine, sugar, lime or lemon juice, and baking powder. Mix all thoroughly, place in a buttered mould, and steam for two hours. To be served with sweet sauce. The bread is better rubbed through a wire sieve before mixing.

TO MAKE YEAST.

INGREDIENTS.

2 quarts clean water, free from grease.	¾ lb. flour.
	As many hops as can be lifted with the finger ends, or ½ oz.
2 ordinary sized potatoes.	
2 tablespoonsful sugar.	

METHOD.—Put the water in the potato pan after dinner before the pan has been washed, add the potatoes, cut small, the hops and sugar, simmer slowly for 30 minutes. Strain through a sieve, and rub the potatoes through into the liquor, throw away the hops, and leave the liquor to cool slightly before adding the flour, as the flour must not be scalded. Place the yeast in a jar or bottle while warm. Keep it in a warm place until it has worked, which will be in about 30 hours, then keep it in a cool place to stop working. Always leave the cork pretty loose to prevent exploding. Yeast should be made at least every week to be good and strong. ½ pint of old yeast will make the new ready for use in 4 hours, but care must be taken that the old yeast is quite sweet, as the least sourness spoils the new.

TO SET BREAD.

INGREDIENTS.

20 lbs. flour.	As much salt water as will
½ pint yeast.	set a smooth sponge.

METHOD.—(In cold weather). Make a hollow in the centre of the flour. Shake the yeast up well before using it, then pour it into the hollow. Have some water sufficiently hot to make the whole into a warm sponge. Sea water makes better bread than fresh water, and requires no salt. If the yeast is good and strong, and the sponge is kept lukewarm, the dough will be ready for turning out in four hours. The right time to put the bread into tins is when the sponge begins to crack on the top. Leave the dough to rise in the tins until the tops begin to crack again. Bottom heat is required first and a moderate oven.

PORRIDGE.

INGREDIENTS.

2 quarts of water.
½ lb. oatmeal.
1 teaspoonful salt.

METHOD.—Have the water boiling, add the salt, sprinkle the oatmeal into the water gradually, whisk well the whole time until all is added. Simmer, well covered, for one hour.

TO MAKE COFFEE. (CREW'S).

INGREDIENTS.

10 ozs. coffee.	20 pints water.

METHOD.— Place the coffee in a bag made of white bunting. Put it in a coffee boiler with the cold water. Leave it in until the water comes to the boil, take the boiler off the fire and leave the bag standing in the hot water for 10 minutes, then take it out and throw away the coffee. Should the coffee be left in the water longer than 10 minutes, the bitterness from the coffee grounds will spoil all. This process should be followed in making tea, keeping separate bags for each.

TO MAKE COCOA.

INGREDIENTS.

1 teaspoonful of cocoa to 1 breakfast cup of water.

METHOD.—Mix the cocoa into a thick paste with cold water or milk, pour over the boiling water and stir well.

BEEF TEA.

INGREDIENTS.

½ lb. lean beef.
½ pint water.
Pinch of salt.

METHOD.—Scrape or cut the meat as small as possible. Put it into an earthenware basin. Pour over the cold water, and cover with paper turned tightly round the edges. Place in the bottom of a slow oven for 1 hour, add salt, and strain off.

GRUEL.

INGREDIENTS.

1 quart of water.
3 tablespoonsful oatmeal.
A pinch of salt.

METHOD.—Have the water boiling, sprinkle in the oatmeal, and whisk it well until it boils, simmer slowly for 1 hour, then strain through a gravy strainer and serve.

CUNJI WATER FOR AN INVALID.

INGREDIENTS.

1 quart fresh water.
3 tablespoonsful Indian rice.

1 teaspoonful lime or lemon juice.
½ teaspoonful salt.

METHOD.—Wash the rice and simmer it in the water for one hour. Strain the water off, skim off any scum that may form, add the salt and leave it to cool. When cold, add the lemon or lime juice.

SEA PIE (FOR 10 MEN).

INGREDIENTS.

15 lbs. potatoes.	4 lbs. cold salt beef or pork.
2 or 3 onions.	2 or 3 carrots, or 2 ozs. preserved
5 lbs flour.	vegetables.
1 lb. suet or dripping.	9 quarts water
A little cayenne.	1 tablespoonful baking powder.

Salt and pepper.

METHOD.—Peel, and cut up the potatoes; lay in a pan. and just cover them with water. Cut up the meat into about ½-inch squares, and place it upon the potatoes. Add the chopped onions and sliced vegetables, cayenne, salt and pepper. Set on the fire to boil.

FOR THE CRUST.—Mix together the flour, salt, and baking powder. Add the finely-chopped suet, or rub in the dripping if dripping is used. Mix to a stiff paste with cold water; roll it out so as to fit the top of the pan. Lay the crust carefully over the meat and potatoes. Simmer gently 2 hours.

DEVILLED BONES.

INGREDIENTS.

Bones of cold joint of beef, mutton, or veal.	Pinch of cayenne.
1 tablespoonful flour.	2 tablespoonfuls butter.
2 tablespoonsful mustard.	2 tablespoonsful Yorkshire Relish
½-pint water.	1 tablespoonful vinegar.
	Pepper and salt.

METHOD.—Chop the bones into neat pieces, having plenty of meat attached to each piece of bone. Fry the pieces in hot dripping till nicely brown. Place in the oven to keep hot. Put into a stewpan the butter and flour, cook till slightly brown, then add the water very gradually stirring all the time. Add all the other ingredients; boil up and pour over the bones just before serving.

POTATO STEW.

INGREDIENTS.

5 lbs. potatoes, 1 lb. cold salt beef or pork, 1 onion, pepper, salt, 1 quart water.

METHOD.—Wash, peel and cut the potatoes into quarters; lay them in a stewpan with the meat, cut in slices, on the top; add the onions cut small, cover and simmer slowly one hour.

PLUM PUDDING.

INGREDIENTS.

1½ lbs. stale bread.	Rind and juice of 1 lemon.
1 oz. candied peel.	6 ozs. currants.
6 tablespoonsful brown sugar.	6 ozs. Valencia raisins.
4 tablespoonsful finely chopped suet.	1 teaspoonful mixed spice
	½ teaspoonful carbonate of soda.

METHOD.—Steep the bread for 20 minutes in cold water. Squeeze it as dry as possible in a clean cloth. Put the bread into a bowl; add the chopped suet, cleaned currants, stoned raisins, and all the other ingredients. Put into a well-greased pudding mould, cover with greased paper, and steam for 3 hours. Serve with brandy sauce.

INVALID CUSTARD.

INGREDIENTS.

½ pint milk, 2 eggs, 1 tablespoonful white sugar.

METHOD.—Beat up the eggs and sugar, add the milk and mix well. Strain into a buttered basin, cover with buttered paper. Steam or bake in very moderate oven, ¾ hr. Let it stand to cool a few minutes, then turn out of the basin.

LEMONADE FOR AN INVALID.

INGREDIENTS.—1½ large lemons, 1 pint boiling water, 1 tablespoonful sugar.

METHOD.--Rub the lemon with a clean cloth to remove the dust. Peel the yellow rind off as thinly as possible—none of the white should be used, as it gives the lemonade a bitter taste. Put the rind with the sugar into a jar. Cut the lemons in half, and squeeze the juice through a strainer into the jar. Pour in the boiling water, cover, set aside till cold, and then strain it.

TOMATO SAUCE FOR CUTLETS.

INGREDIENTS.

½ lb. tinned tomatoes.	Cayenne, pepper and salt.
2 ozs. butter.	A pinch of sugar.
1 oz. flour.	1 teaspoonful vinegar.
¼ pint water or stock.	

METHOD.—Put the butter and flour into a saucepan, brown slightly, add the water gradually, stirring all the time. Add the other ingredients. Simmer 20 minutes. Rub through a wire sieve. Re-heat, and serve round cutlets or in a sauce boat.

SECOND COURSE.

GRAVY SOUP.

INGREDIENTS.

4 quarts fresh stock.	3 bay leaves.
4 ozs. dripping.	1 teaspoonful pepper.
4 tablespoonsful flour.	6 eschalots or 2 small onions.
6 cloves.	1 teaspoonful brown sugar.
1 small carrot.	1 teaspoonful vinegar.
2 blades of mace.	1 teaspoonful salt.

METHOD.—Make the dripping hot in a stew pan and brown the sliced onions. Brown the flour well, add stock gradually, then all the other ingredients, and simmer slowly for 40 minutes. Strain through a sieve and remove all fat. Re-heat and serve.

FISH CAKES.

INGREDIENTS.

1 lb. cooked fish.	1 teaspoonful mustard.
3 lbs. potatoes.	1 teaspoonful anchovy sauce.
1 small onion.	Salt to taste.
½ teaspoonful pepper.	

METHOD.—Remove all bones and skin from the fish, and mince it finely. Boil the potatoes, dry them well, and add the fish and onion, chopped finely, the anchovy, mustard, and pepper. Mash all thoroughly, leaving no lumps of potatoes, mould it into cakes, flouring them outside. Brown in hot fat. Take care to have no flour but on the outside of the cakes. They may be moulded and dipped into a rather thick batter of flour and water, then covered with crumbs with a little parsley in them, and fried in hot fat.

SALT FISH CHOWDER.

INGREDIENTS.

1 lb. cooked fish.	1 tablespoonful flour.
2 lbs. potatoes.	1 pint fresh milk or water.
1 small onion.	½ teaspoonful white pepper.
1 thin slice of bacon.	Salt as required.
1 tablespoonful butter.	

METHOD.—Remove the skin and bones from the fish, and break it into large flakes. Wash, peel, and cut the potatoes in halves or quarters. Mince the onion finely, put the butter in the pan to warm, add the flour and mix well, add milk or water gradually, and half the potatoes, all the fish, onion, bacon cut small, and pepper. Put the remaining potatoes over the fish, &c., and simmer slowly for forty minutes. Before serving, sprinkle chopped parsley over all.

SALT FISH AND EGG SAUCE.

INGREDIENTS.

2 lbs. salt cod fish.	2 tablespoonsful butter.
1 egg.	½ pint water or fresh milk.
2 tablespoonsful flour.	

METHOD.—Cut the fish into small squares, leaving the under skin to keep the fish together. Steep it for 4 hours in salt water, then boil for 40 minutes in fresh water and drain.

EGG SAUCE.

Put the butter in a saucepan, slightly warm, add the flour and mix thoroughly to smooth batter, add boiling water gradually. Boil an egg for 20 minutes, then chop it finely, and add it to the sauce. Pour all over the fish and serve.

HARICOT MUTTON.

INGREDIENTS.

2 lbs. neck of mutton.	1 tablespoonful flour.
1 ordinary sized carrot.	2 tablespoonsful dripping.
4 small onions.	1 pint of water.
4 cloves.	Pepper and salt, as required.
1 tablespoonful piccalilli.	

METHOD.—Cut the mutton into thick fillets, and fry them brown in hot fat; take them out, leaving two tablespoonsful of fat in the stew pan. In this brown the flour, and add the water gradually. Put the mutton at the bottom of the pan, and add the carrots cut into shapes, with the onions sliced, the cloves, pepper, salt, and piccalilli. simmer for one hour. Take the cloves out before serving, and garnish with parsley.

MUTTON AND POTATO PIE.

INGREDIENTS.

1 lb. rough chops.	1 teaspoonful flour.
1 lb. potatoes.	¼ teaspoonful pepper.
1 small onion.	A little cold water and salt.

METHOD.—Cut the mutton chops into 2 or 3 pieces, slightly coat them with flour, pepper and salt mixed together. Put the chops in a pie dish, chop the onion into small pieces, and sprinkle over the mutton. Cut the potatoes into thick half slices, and lay them over all. Nearly fill the dish with water, and cover with suet puff paste. Bake quickly to cook the pastry first. Take out of the oven, and set on the range to finish cooking the meat and potatoes. Meat pies must be ventilated to allow the gases to escape, and keep the crust in position.

GRILLED BONES.

INGREDIENTS.

2 lbs. cold meat bones.	¼ pint cold water.
1 tablespoonful dripping.	Pepper, salt, and cayenne.
1 tablespoonful flour.	

METHOD.—Take cold beef bones with plenty of meat attached; chop them in two-inch lengths; fry them brown in hot fat. Make a brown gravy with a tablespoonful of hot fat, and the same of flour, well coloured; add water or stock gradually; season highly, and pour over the bones on a dish.

SIRLOIN OF ROAST BEEF.

To roast beef in the oven dredge a little flour all over. Baste the joint all over with hot dripping before placing in hot oven; this is to close the pores of the meat. Time according to size of joint and heat of the oven. To be served with Yorkshire pudding or roast potatoes.

YORKSHIRE PUDDING.

INGREDIENTS.

1 pint fresh milk.	A pinch of salt.
2 eggs.	¼ lb. flour.

METHOD.—Whip the eggs very lightly, add the milk and salt, pour it gradually on to the flour, and beat well. Put it into a well-greased tin and bake one hour. Pour over it some of the beef dripping, and bake again for 10 minutes. Serve it round the beef in slices.

MINCED COLLOPS.

INGREDIENTS.

2 lbs. lean tender beef.	1 tablespoonful butter.
2 small onions.	1 teaspoonful salt.
½ bunch sweet herbs.	3 gills of water.
1 large tablespoonful flour.	Pepper as required.

METHOD.—Cut the meat and onions finely, sprinkle the herbs over the meat. Fry the onions brown in hot butter, then brown the flour, add the water gradually, and put in the meat and other ingredients. Simmer 40 minutes, keeping the pan well covered. Garnish with toasted bread and parsley.

CURRIED PRESERVED MUTTON.
(Cold Meat Cookery).

INGREDIENTS.

1 lb. tinned roast mutton.	1 teaspoonful salt.
2 small onions.	1 teaspoonful vinegar.
1 tablespoonful butter or dripping.	½ teaspoonful sugar.
1 tablespoonful curry powder.	2 potatoes.
1 teaspoonful flour.	½ pint of water.

METHOD.—Break the mutton in pieces. Make the butter hot in a stew-pan ; cut the onions small and brown them, take them out and mix in the flour and curry powder, add the water gradually, and, when simmering, add the potatoes cut into small dice shapes, the mutton, onion, vinegar, salt, and sugar. Simmer about 20 minutes.

RISSOLES.
(Cold Meat Cookery.)

INGREDIENTS.

1 lb. cold beef or mutton, without fat.	A little sweet herbs and chopped parsley.
1 small onion, cooked.	Crushed vermicelli or bread crumbs.
2 tablespoonsful flour.	Salt as required.
2 tablespoonsful steeped bread.	
¼ teaspoonful white pepper.	

METHOD.—Mince the meat and onion finely, add the bread after steeping and pressing well ; then pepper, salt, and herbs ; make into small cakes ; dip into a rather thick batter of flour and water ; toss in crushed vermicelli or crumbs ; and brown in hot fat.

To be served with brown gravy and mashed potatoes.

CROQUETTES OF SALT BEEF.
(*Cold Meat Cookery.*)

INGREDIENTS.

1 lb. cooked salt beef.	2 tablespoonsful bread, steeped.
1 small onion.	Little sweet herbs and pepper.
1 tablespoonful flour.	A pinch of spice.

METHOD.—Mince the meat finely, strain and squeeze the bread dry, mix all the ingredients thoroughly, and make into small rolls all the same size, flour them slightly, dip into rather thick batter of flour and water, cover with bread crumbs and fry in plenty of hot fat.

To be served with brown gravy.

SAUSAGE ROLLS.
(*Cold Meat Cookery.*)

INGREDIENTS.

1 lb. cold meat, fresh, salt or tinned.	2 tablespoonsful steeped bread.
	½ teaspoonful pepper.
1 ordinary sized onion.	Pinch of sweet herbs.

FOR PASTRY.

1½ lbs. flour.	Cold water and salt.
½ lb. dripping or lard.	

METHOD.—Place the flour in the mixing bowl, break the dripping or lard into small lumps and rub them into the flour, add the salt and mix into a dough with cold water. Roll the pastry out twice and leave it to cool. Mince the meat finely, and par-boil the onions before mincing them. If salt meat is used scald it after mincing, add the herbs and seasoning. Mix with the steeped bread well squeezed. Mould into sausages. Lay them on thin sheets of pastry and join the edges by slightly wetting them. Make all the same size and brush over with egg. Bake in a moderate oven one hour.

HASHED MUTTON.
(*Cold Meat Cookery*).

INGREDIENTS.

1 lb. cooked mutton.	1 dessertspoonful dripping.
1 small onion.	½ pint water.
1 dessertspoonful flour.	Pepper, salt, and a pinch of sugar.

METHOD.—Make the dripping hot in a stewpan. Brown the onion sliced, brown the flour, and add the water gradually. Keep stirring until it boils, then add the mutton, cut in rather large pieces. Simmer slowly for forty minutes, and add the seasoning ten minutes before serving.

DEVILLED BEEF.

(Cold Meat Cookery.)

INGREDIENTS.

1 lb. cold beef.	½ pint water.
1 teaspoonful flour.	1 teaspoonful vinegar.
1 dessertspoonful mustard.	½ teaspoonful sugar.
1 tablespoonful Yorkshire relish.	A dust of pepper.
1 oz. butter.	Salt.

METHOD.—Heat the butter in a stew-pan, add the dry mustard and flour and simmer for a few seconds, then add water, pepper, sugar, relish, and salt. Cut the beef in thin fillets, fry them brown, and add them to the gravy. Simmer in covered pan for 30 minutes.

GOLDEN PUDDING.

INGREDIENTS.

½ lb. bread crumbs.	4 tablespoonful sugar.
6 ozs. suet.	½ teaspoonful powdered ginger.
½ lb. marmalade.	Squeeze of lemon or lime
2 eggs.	juice.

METHOD.—Chop the suet very fine, and mix it with the bread crumbs, sugar, ginger, and marmalade; beat the eggs lightly and pour them over the ingredients, and mix to smooth dough. Put into a buttered mould and steam for 2 hours.

To be served with sweet lemon sauce.

QUEEN OF PUDDINGS.

INGREDIENTS.

1 pint of bread crumbs.	2 eggs.
4 tablespoonsful sugar.	1 teaspoonful lime juice.
2 tablespoonsful butter.	¼ lb. jam.
1 pint milk.	

METHOD.—Put the crumbs into a buttered pie dish; boil the milk, butter, and sugar, pour over the crumbs; sprinkle with the lime juice, and leave it to soak. Beat up the yolks of two eggs and pour these over all. Bake till set. Spread the top with the jam, beat the whites of the eggs to a stiff froth, add one teaspoonful of powdered sugar after whipping, pour it over the jam lightly. Put in the oven to slightly brown. The eggs must not be old or packed in salt, as these can seldom be whipped sufficiently to stand.

CORN FLOUR MOULD.

INGREDIENTS.

1 pint of milk.	1 tablespoonful butter.
3 tablespoonsful corn flour.	10 drops of vanilla essence.
2 tablespoonsful white sugar.	

METHOD.—Put the milk, sugar, essence and butter into a stewpan to boil. Mix the corn flour with a little cold water and pour it into the boiling milk, keeping it well stirred with a wire whisk. Boil for five minutes, and pour it into a cold, wet jelly mould. When set turn it on to a glass dish, and garnish it with stewed fruit.

MANISTY PUDDING.

INGREDIENTS.

1 pint of bread crumbs.	1 candied peel.
3 ozs. suet.	Grated rind of 2 lemons.
3 tablespoonsful currants.	Enough water to make dough.
3 tablespoonsful sugar.	½ teaspoonful carbonate of
3 tablespoonsful flour.	soda.

METHOD.—Chop the suet finely, wash and dry the currants, and chop the candied peel fine. Mix all the ingredients together thoroughly, and add enough water to make a stiff mixture. Put into a well buttered mould and steam for 2 hours.

To be served with sweet sauce.

BREAD AND BUTTER PUDDING.

INGREDIENTS.

1 lb. stale bread.	2 tablespoonsful butter.
1 pint condensed milk (mixed).	1 egg.
2 tablespoonsful sugar.	Squeeze of lemon or lime juice.
2 tablespoonsful washed currants.	

METHOD.—Cut the bread into thin slices, all one size, to suit the pie dish. Dip them into water and put them in layers in the pie dish and sprinkle with the currants. Beat together the milk, egg, sugar, and lemon juice; pour it over the bread; add the butter, divided into four pieces; and bake one hour in the bottom of a moderate oven.

RICE FRITTERS.

INGREDIENTS.

1 lb. cooked rice.	A pinch of sugar.
2 tablespoonsful flour.	1 egg if possible.
1 teaspoonful salt.	A pinch of baking powder.
A little cayenne pepper.	

METHOD.—Have the rice well cooked, add the flour, salt, cayenne, and baking powder. Beat up the egg very lightly, and mix all to a firm batter, or if made without egg, add a little water for moisture. Fry in spoonsful, dipping the spoon into the fat to prevent the mixture sticking to the spoon; make the batter thick enough to keep in shape.

PUFF PASTE WITH SUET.

INGREDIENTS.

1 lb. flour.	A little salt if fresh suet is used.
14 ozs. suet.	Cold water.

METHOD.—Make a smooth dough with flour and water. Take away all skins and fibres from the suet, and press it well with the rolling pin, working it up to the consistency of butter. Roll out the pastry. Add the suet in lumps. Fold and roll out 3 times, taking care to thoroughly mix the suet with the dough in the three rolls. Leave it to set for half-hour before using. Bake in a quick oven.

ROUGH PUFF PASTE.

INGREDIENTS.

1 lb. flour.	8 ozs. firm butter.
4 ozs. lard or dripping.	Cold water.

METHOD.—Cut the dripping or lard in small pieces and mix it with the flour; add enough cold water to make a light dough. Roll it out thinly, add the butter with a cold knife, double the pastry over it, and roll very lightly, three times. Leave it to stand in a cool place half-an-hour before using.

LIGHT CAKES WITH CONDENSED MILK.

INGREDIENTS.

1 pint of milk.	1 lb. flour.
1 pint of water.	1 teaspoonful salt.
$\frac{1}{4}$ pint of yeast.	

METHOD.—Place the flour in a mixing bowl with the salt. Add the milk and yeast, and the lukewarm water. Make the whole into warm batter, and set it to rise about 3 hours in a warm place well covered. When ready have some pastry tins greased. Make them hot on the top of the range, drop in sufficient batter to spread evenly round. Place the cakes at a little distance apart, and bake on the top of the stove, turning with knife when thoroughly set.

VICTORIA SANDWICHES.

INGREDIENTS.

5 eggs.	Juice of half a lemon.
3 tablespoonsful fine white sugar.	1 teaspoonful baking powder.
5 tablespoonsful flour.	6 ozs. jam.
3 ozs. butter.	

METHOD.—Beat the butter and sugar to a cream, and add the lemon juice. Beat the eggs separately until very light, add them to the butter and sugar, and dredge in the flour gradually, beat all together for 10 minutes, then add the baking powder just before the batter is ready for the oven. Pour into small well-buttered sandwich tins, and bake brown for 15 to 20 minutes, according to the heat of the oven, which must be quick. Turn out, and, when cold, cut into two slices, spread jam over one piece, lay the other piece over and cut into fingers. Dust over with fine white sugar and serve in a pyramid.

CHESTER CAKES.

INGREDIENTS.

2 ozs. steeped bread.	1 tablespoonful butter or lard.
½ lb. currants.	1 candied peel.
½ lb. Valencia raisins.	2 apples or same size of Swede
6 tablespoonsful sugar.	turnips.

FOR CRUST.

1½ lbs. flour.	Little cold water and salt.
10 ozs. dripping.	

METHOD.—Wash and pick the currants, stone the raisins and chop them with the apples or turnips, cut the candied peel very small, and squeeze the water well out of the bread, then mix all the ingredients together. Make a light paste with the flour, dripping and water. Roll out into two square sheets, both the same size and not too thin. Lay one on a baking tin, spread the mixture evenly over leaving the edges clear, and wet the edge all round. Lay on the cover, press the edges together and prick with a fork. Bake well, cut into squares, and arrange in a pyramid.

SARDINE FRITTERS.

METHOD.—Open the sardine tin as near the top as possible. Turn the fish out without breaking, drain off the oil, and drop the sardines into batter, as for bacon fritters. Fry them brown in a bath of fat. The white of one egg well whipped and added lightly to batter makes these fritters more crisp.

POTATO CHIPS WITH BACON.

METHOD.—Wash, peel, and chip potatoes all the same length and thickness. Have plenty of hot fat. Wipe the potatoes as dry as possible and place them in the fat, taking care it well covers the potatoes. The fat must be very hot and over a good fire. When nicely browned turn out, sprinkle with salt, and shake well. Serve with bacon fried for garnish.

BACON FRITTERS WITHOUT EGGS.

INGREDIENTS.

½ lb. cooked lean bacon.	½ teaspoonful salt.
½ lb. flour.	Enough cold water to make
1 teaspoonful baking powder.	batter.

METHOD.—Cut the bacon into 14 small fillets. Mix together the salt, flour, and baking powder, and add enough cold water to make it into a firm batter. Cover the pieces of bacon with the batter, and drop each piece of bacon in very hot fat, fry a nice brown, taking care all are the same size. The batter must on no account be too thin, and the fat must be thoroughly hot to prevent the batter running.

BEEF BRAWN.

INGREDIENTS.

4 lbs. thin beef.	½ bunch thyme.
4 bay leaves.	8 pepper corns.
6 cloves.	Salt as required and water.

METHOD.—Cut the meat into one inch squares, and remove all the fat and gristle. Place it in a stew pan, with enough water to just cover it. Add the herbs, cloves, and pepper in a piece of muslin, and simmer slowly for 3½ hours. Remove the herbs after the first hour. Skim off any fat, taking care not to break the pieces of meat. When tender, add salt, and pour all into a tin or plain mould and leave this to set in a cool place.

THIRD COURSE.

JULIENNE SOUP.

INGREDIENTS.

3 quarts clear stock.	A little chopped parsley.
2 tablespoonsful butter.	1 lettuce.
1 teaspoonful sugar.	2 small onions.
½ teaspoonful vinegar.	4 cloves.
1 ordinary sized carrot.	1 slice of thin toasted bread.
1 small turnip.	Salt and pepper.

METHOD.—Make the butter hot and fry in it one onion, carrot and turnip, which should be cut in thin, narrow strips about 1¼ inches long. Add the stock and simmer for 20 minutes, adding the second onion with the cloves stuck in it. Skim off the scum and fat, then add the lettuce cut rather large, the sugar, vinegar, pepper and salt. Lay small pieces of toast and chopped parsley in the tureen, pour the boiling soup over, and serve.

TOMATO SOUP.

INGREDIENTS.

2 quarts stock.	1 tablespoonful vinegar.
3 lbs. tomatoes.	6 cloves.
3 tablespoonsful dripping.	2 lumps of sugar.
3 tablespoonsful flour.	2 small onions, pepper and salt.

METHOD.—Heat the dripping in a stew pan, and brown in it the flour, add the stock gradually, also the tomatoes (cut in two), onions, cloves, salt, pepper, and sugar, and allow the soup to simmer for one hour. Rub it through a fine wire sieve, skim off the fat, reheat it and serve, adding the vinegar in the tureen.

VERMICELLI SOUP.

INGREDIENTS.

2 quarts stock.	1 ham bone.
1 small onion.	1½ ozs. vermicelli.
1 bayleaf.	White of one egg.
4 cloves.	Pepper, cayenne.

METHOD.—Boil the vermicelli for 15 minutes in half pint of the stock, with the onion, cloves, and bayleaf. Remove these seasonings, and boil the rest of the stock with the bone and the well-whipped white of the egg for 40 minutes, skimming occasionally. Colour the soup with caramel, if liked, add the vermicelli, season, and serve with a little chopped parsley.

SPRING SOUP.

INGREDIENTS.

2 quarts stock.	¼ pint green peas.
1 small spring carrot.	1 white of egg.
1 small spring turnip.	2 pieces of loaf sugar.
6 small spring onions.	1 tablespoonful dripping, pepper,
1 small spring lettuce.	salt, chopped parsley.

METHOD.—Heat the dripping in a stew pan, cut the carrot and turnips into small pieces and fry them brown in the dripping, to colour the soup. Add the stock gradually with the white of egg beaten well into the stock. Simmer for 20 minutes, skimming off all fat and scum ; add the other ingredients (the lettuce and onions being cut small) and simmer slowly for 30 minutes longer, and skim again. Serve with chopped parsley sprinkled over the soup in the tureen.

MUTTON PUDDING.

INGREDIENTS.

1½ lbs. mutton.	3 ozs. suet.
1 small onion.	1 teaspoonful salt.
¼ pint water.	½ teaspoonful pepper.
10 tablespoonsful flour.	

METHOD.—Chop the suet, removing all skin ; mix it well with the flour and a pinch of salt ; add enough cold water to make it into a firm dough, and roll out once. Grease a pudding mould well, and line it with the pastry, leaving enough dough to cover the pudding. Cut the mutton into rather large pieces, roll them in flour, pepper, and salt mixed. Put the mutton into the mould, and add quarter pint of water. Wet the edges of the paste, and cover it. Cover with greased paper, and steam in a closely covered pan for 2 hours.

BEEF OLIVES.

INGREDIENTS.

2 lbs. rump steak.	1 teaspoonful mixed herbs.
¼ lb. bacon.	a little cayenne, also pepper, and
2 tablespoonsful bread crumbs.	½ teaspoonful salt.
	1 onion.

METHOD.—Cut the steak into 8 thin fillets, as nearly as possible of one size, about 2½ inches square. Cut the bacon thinly and lay one piece on each fillet. Chop together very finely the trimmings of the meat and the bacon, add the crumbs slightly damped, the herbs, salt, pepper, and the finely-chopped onion. Put a little of this stuffing on each fillet, and roll them up into sausage shapes. Run 2 skewers through all to fasten them together, trim the ends and fry them brown in hot fat

Make ½ pint of brown gravy, nicely seasoned, in a stew pan, lay in the olives, and allow them to simmer slowly for 1 hour with the pan closely covered.

Serve with green olives in the gravy.

GRILLED STEAK.

Steak or chops must be grilled over quick, bright fire. If done on the range it is best to remove the hot plate nearest the fire. Slightly grease the grill before placing meat over the fire to keep meat from sticking to the bars. If the meat is not sufficiently cooked through, place in oven a few seconds after seasoning, before sending it to table. All meats to be grilled must be thicker than for frying.

CURRIED MUTTON.

INGREDIENTS.

1 lb. mutton.	1 teaspoonful flour.
1 small onion.	1 oz. butter or dripping.
1 large potato or small apple.	½ pint water.
1 large tablespoonful curry powder.	Salt as required.

METHOD.—Cut the mutton and potato into pieces the size of a small nut. Make the butter hot in the stew pan and fry the mutton and potato brown. Remove them and leave enough fat in the pan to brown the onion. Add the curry powder and flour, and simmer for one minute, stirring with an iron spoon. Add the water gradually and boil, then add the meat and seasoning, and simmer slowly for 40 minutes. One teaspoonful of vinegar and a pinch of sugar improves the flavour.

MUTTON CUTLETS.

INGREDIENTS.

2 lbs. mutton cutlets.	1 teaspoonful butter.
½ teaspoonful salt.	1 egg.
¼ teaspoonful pepper.	Crumbs and parsley.

METHOD.– Cut the cutlets thin, leaving the ends of the bones well scraped to the depth of half an inch. Flatten them and make all the same size and length; dip each into egg, season with pepper and salt, and toss in crumbs and chopped parsley. Fry in hot dripping a good brown colour. Serve hot with brown gravy. Cutlets must not lie flat on a dish but stand on end, clear of the gravy.

BEEF CUTLETS.

INGREDIENTS.

2 lbs. of beef fillets.	Salt and pepper.
1 egg.	1 teaspoonful of flour.
A little chopped parsley.	Bread crumbs.
2 teaspoonsful water.	

METHOD.—Cut the fillets into nice thin steaks all the same size and shape. Slightly dust with pepper and salt; beat up the egg, flour and water together, dip the cutlets into the batter, and coat all over with crumbs and parsley mixed. Fry a nice rich brown in plenty of hot fat. Place them on the top of mashed potatoes in an entrée dish.

Serve with brown gravy or tomato sauce, and garnish with fried parsley.

STEWED STEAK AND ONIONS.

INGREDIENTS.

2 lbs. beef steak.	½ teaspoonful white pepper.
2 tablespoonsful dripping.	½ teaspoonful salt.
2 tablespoonsful flour.	1 pint water.
2 good-sized onions.	2 cloves.

METHOD.– Cut the steak into nice fillets and brown them in the hot dripping, remove the meat, cut the onions in slices and brown them, stir in the flour, allow it also to brown, then add the water gradually, and simmer the gravy for five minutes, keeping it well stirred, add the meat, seasoning, and cloves, and simmer 20 minutes. Take out the cloves and serve.

VOL-AU-VENT OF KIDNEY.

INGREDIENTS.

½ lb. of puff pastry.	1 teaspoonful butter.
1 beef kidney.	¼ pint of water.
½ small onion, sliced.	A pinch of spice, pepper and salt.
1 teaspoonful flour.	A pinch of sweet herbs.

METHOD.—Roll out the pastry half an inch thick. Cut it in oval shape and stamp the centre for the lid. Bake it in a quick oven to a nice brown, take off the centre, and draw out some of the crumb from inside, leaving space enough for the kidney. Cut the kidney small, make the butter hot in a stew pan, and brown in it the onion and kidney. Remove these and brown the flour, add the water gradually, then add the kidney, herbs, spice, pepper and salt, and simmer one hour. Pour it into the pastry case, cover with the lid, and serve. Garnish with parsley.

SHEEP'S TONGUES IN ASPIC.

INGREDIENTS.

1 tin of sheep's tongues.

1 pint aspic jelly.

METHOD.—Turn the tongues out of the tin without breaking, and remove all fat and jelly. Put aspic to the depth of half-an-inch at the bottom of a plain mould, large enough to hold the tongues. When this is quite set, lay in the tongues, pour over the aspic, and set aside till cold. When ready to turn out dip the mould once in hot water, wipe off the drops and turn it over on a dish. Garnish with parsley or fresh salad. The jelly must be liquid, but quite cold when poured over the tongues, for if the least warm it will melt the fat and become cloudy.

BEEF CROQUETTES.

(Cold Meat Cookery.)

INGREDIENTS.

1½ lbs. minced beef.	½ teaspoonful salt.
1 small onion.	Yolk of 1 egg.
½ teaspoonful white pepper.	Sweet herbs.

METHOD.—Half cook the onion and mince it finely. Mix all the ingredients together, and make into 10 small sausage shapes. Dip them into egg, or flour and water, crumb them, and fry brown in plenty of hot fat.

To be served with brown gravy and mashed potatoes on an entrée dish.

POTATOES À LA MAITRE D'HOTEL.

INGREDIENTS.

2 lbs. potatoes.	2 cloves.
1 teaspoonful chopped parsley.	½ bay leaf.
½ pint good clear stock.	Squeeze of lemon juice.
1 tablespoonful flour.	½ teaspoonful condensed milk.
1 tablespoonful butter.	A little cayenne and pepper.

METHOD.— Choose the potatoes all the same size. Wash, peel, and place them in boiling water. Cook tender with a little salt, but do not break them. Place the stock in a stew pan, add the bay leaf, cloves, salt and cayenne, and simmer 10 minutes well covered. Make the butter hot in saucepan, add flour, and stir well, but do not colour; strain stock to flour and butter, and make a smooth sauce. Add milk and chopped parsley, and pour it over the potatoes in a side dish.

SCALLOPED LIVER.
(*Cold Meat Cookery.*)
INGREDIENTS.

1 lb. cold liver.	Sweet herbs.
1 small onion.	Salt and pepper.
1 tablespoonful dripping.	¼ pint of water.
1 tablespoonful flour.	

METHOD.—Mince the liver and onions small, separately. Make the dripping hot in a stew pan. Brown the onion and flour. Add the water gradually, keeping it well stirred until simmering, then add the liver, herbs, pepper, and salt, and simmer slowly for 20 minutes. Serve with sippets of toast.

SCOTCH CHEESE CAKES.
INGREDIENTS.

½ lb. puff paste.	3 tablespoonsful flour.
¼ lb. jam.	1 oz. butter.
3 eggs.	4 drops essence of almonds.
3 teaspoonsful sugar.	1 teaspoonful baking powder.

METHOD.—Line eight small patty tins with thin puff paste, and drop into the centre of each a small teaspoonful of jam.

Beat the butter and sugar to a cream, add the eggs and flour alternately, beating well, then add the essence and lastly the baking powder. Drop a good spoonful into each tin taking care to cover the jam, but only three parts filling the tins. Make little open knots of the trimmings of the pastry, dropping one knot on to the top of the batter in each, and bake in a moderate oven for about 25 minutes.

SEMOLINA PUDDING.

INGREDIENTS.

2 dessertspoonsful semolina.	1 tablespoonful moist sugar.
1 pint milk.	¼ teaspoonful vanilla.
Pinch of salt.	2 eggs.

METHOD.—Put the semolina into a pan with the milk and salt, let it stand ten minutes. Set it on the fire, stir till it boils, continue to stir for ten minutes, be careful not to let it burn, set aside for a few minutes. Stir in the sugar, vanilla, and the yolks of two eggs. Beat up the whites of the eggs to a stiff froth, stir lightly in. Butter a dish, pour in, and bake for 20 minutes.

FRUIT JELLY.

INGREDIENTS.

4 oranges.	¼ pint of sherry.
4 tablespoonsful white sugar.	¾ oz. gelatine.
1 pint of water.	

METHOD.—Grate the rind of oranges finely. Peel the white pith. Cut the oranges into slices and place in a stew pan with the sugar and grated rind. Steep the gelatine for 20 minutes in the pint of water, put all on the fire, and simmer, well covered, for 30 minutes. Strain through a jelly bag, and pour into a cold wet mould. Take care not to turn out of the mould before it is thoroughly cold.

In hot weather allow 1 oz. of gelatine.

COMPOTE OF FRUIT AND RICE.

INGREDIENTS.

1 bottle of plums.	½ lb. Patna rice.
6 tablespoons of white sugar.	2 quarts of water.
10 drops essence of ratafia.	

METHOD.—Boil the rice quickly for 20 minutes, strain it into a colander, and leave it to drain. Sprinkle 2 tablespoons of sugar over it and shake it to mix well. Mould it with a wet wine-glass or cup, and turn out on a glass dish in a ring, leaving a space in the centre for the fruit. Colour a little crystallized sugar with one drop of carmine or cochineal to ornament the moulds. Pour the plums into a basin, without breaking the fruit. Pour the juice into a stew pan with the sugar, and essence, and boil to a syrup. Place the plums in the centre of the rice moulds, and pour the juice over them when cool.

BLANC-MANGE. (Two colours.)

INGREDIENTS.

1½ pints of milk, fresh or condensed.	3 drops almond essence.
6 tablespoonsful white sugar.	6 drops cochineal or carmine.
10 drops vanilla essence.	¼ lb. corn flour.
	¼ pint water.

(For the coloured.)

METHOD.—Have a jelly mould steeping in cold fresh water. Put the water in a saucepan, add the cochineal or carmine, one tablespoonful of sugar, and three drops of almond essence. Mix one good tablespoonful corn flour with a little water, and when the cochineal water comes to the boil, add the corn flour. Whisk well. Pour into the wet mould, taking care to drop it in the centre of the mould so as to set even. Leave it to cool until the white is ready.

(For the white.)

METHOD.—Put one pint of milk into another saucepan, add the sugar and vanilla. Put on range to boil, keep well stirred. Mix remaining corn flour with remaining milk; pour this in the pan, whisk well, and pour into jelly mould on top of the red, taking care that it is well cooked and poured into centre of mould, so as to be evenly set and leave no hollow spaces at the sides. Leave it to set until properly cold, if possible, on ice. Shake well, before turning out, and garnish with coloured jam.

LEMON CHEESE CAKES.

INGREDIENTS.

4 eggs.	2 ozs. butter.
3 tablespoonsful white sugar.	1 lb. good puff pastry.
2 lemons.	

METHOD.—Break the eggs into a basin, leaving out the whites of two, add the grated rind and juice of the lemons, the sugar, and butter. Beat it well for 10 minutes, then pour it into a jar. Place the jar in a pan of boiling water, stirring the mixture in one direction with a wooden spoon, until the lemon cheese becomes thick enough to stand firm.

Bake the paste in patty tins as for jam tartlets, when well baked and cold, fill them with the lemon cheese.

SWEET OMELET.

INGREDIENTS.

3 eggs.	1 oz. butter.
1 tablespoonful milk.	Jam.
Pinch of salt.	

METHOD.—Separate the yolks and whites of the eggs. Beat the whites to a stiff froth, and mix the yolks, milk, and salt in a large bowl. Melt the butter in an omelet pan, and when hot, but not coloured, stir the whites in with the yolks, and turn instantly into the butter. Stir the mixture gently with a wooden spoon till the butter is worked in, and the eggs begin to set, then let it cook till slightly browned underneath and set. Place the pan quickly under heat to set the top, and when nicely browned, slip a broad knife under the omelet in the middle and lift it folded on to a hot dish, keeping the top outside. Lift the fold and lay between one or two spoonsful of jam, which should be warmed by standing in hot water. To be served very quickly.

GINGER PUDDING.

INGREDIENTS.

1 pint of bread crumbs.	4 tablespoonsful white sugar.
1 dessertspoonful powdered ginger.	1 teaspoonful baking powder.
	2 sticks of preserved ginger.
3 ozs. butter or suet.	The juice of 1 lemon.
2 tablespoonsful flour.	A little water or milk.

METHOD.—Chop the suet fine, removing skin and fibre. Chop the preserved ginger. Mix the dry ingredients together, and add water or milk sufficient to make a firm batter. Put it into a well-buttered mould, and steam for 2 hours.

Bread makes a lighter pudding than flour, and takes less time to cook. To be served with sweet sauce.

SATISFACTION PUDDING.

INGREDIENTS.

10 small sponge cakes.	1 pint milk, fresh or con-
2 tablespoonsful butter	densed.
¼-lb. coloured jam.	3 eggs.
3 tablespoonsful white sugar.	6 drops of essence of vanilla.

METHOD.—Wash the butter well, squeeze out the water and salt in a clean cloth. Butter a large sized pudding mould thickly, taking care that the mould is quite dry. Cut the sponge cakes into long thin pieces, and line the mould with them inside as neatly as possible. Place the jam in the bottom, beat the eggs, sugar, and milk well together, and pour it over the jam, add the essence, and the remaining sponge cake to form a floating cover. Cover all with well buttered paper turned lightly round edges, and steam for two hours. To be served on a silver dish.

PUFF PASTRY WITH BUTTER.

(An easy method for beginners.)

INGREDIENTS.

1 lb. flour.   1 lb. butter.   Cold water.

METHOD.—Break the butter in good sized pieces into cold flour with a cold knife. Cover the butter well with flour and mix together, add enough cold water to make all into dough, taking care not to break the butter. Roll it out lightly. Put it aside to cool for ten minutes, then roll it out again, and put it to cool for ten minutes. Roll it out the third time, and cool for half-an-hour before using. Care must be taken that the butter is not in patches. After the third roll, if the paste is not an even colour all over, roll out again.

SODA SCONES.

INGREDIENTS.

2 lbs. flour.	½ teaspoonful carbonate of
1½ pints fresh milk or water.	soda.
2 dessertspoonsful baking	1 teaspoonful salt.
powder.	

METHOD.—Mix together the flour, salt, baking powder, and carbonate of soda. Add the milk or water gradually until sufficient to make a light dough. Handle it as little as possible, and roll out into a large round cake. Mark it deeply into four, brush over with egg, prick with a fork, and place in a hot oven as soon as possible. Time, 20 minutes.

ROCK CAKES.

INGREDIENTS.

1 lb. flour.	3 teaspoonsful baking powder.
6 ozs. lard or good dripping.	1 teaspoonful powdered ginger.
6 ozs. sugar.	2 eggs.
4 ozs. currants.	1 gill milk or water.
1 large skin of candied peel.	A pinch of salt.

METHOD.—Chop one half of the candied peel, leaving the other for decorating, wash the currants, dry them thoroughly. Mix together all the dry ingredients, make it into a firm dough with the well beaten eggs and the milk. Drop the mixture on greased tins, in rocky shapes, making about twenty-four cakes. Cut the remaining candied peel into twenty-four thin slices, placing one on each bun, and bake in rather a quick oven for about 15 minutes.

QUEEN CAKES.

INGREDIENTS.

4 eggs (as fresh as possible).	5 tablespoonsful flour.
3 tablespoonsful white sugar.	2 ozs. butter.
1 teaspoonful lemon juice.	1 teaspoonful baking powder.

METHOD.—Remove the salt from the butter by washing it in cold water, squeeze in a clean cloth to dry it thoroughly. Beat the butter and sugar to a cream, add the well-beaten eggs, dredge in the flour gradually, and add the lemon juice after all the flour is in, and lastly, add the baking powder. Beat it well, and pour it into well buttered patty tins, into which a few clean, dry currants have been dropped. This batter should be well beaten before adding the powder.

Put the patty pans on to a large baking tin, and bake 15 minutes in a quick oven.

SHORT BREAD.

INGREDIENTS.

1 lb. flour.	$\frac{1}{2}$ oz. sweet almonds.
2 ozs. corn flour.	A few carraway seeds.
$\frac{1}{2}$ lb. butter.	A few thin slices of candied
5 ozs. pounded loaf sugar.	peel.

METHOD.—Whip the butter to a cream, gradually dredge in the flour and the corn flour; also the sugar and carraway seeds. Blanch the almonds and chop them small, add them to the butter and knead the paste for 15 minutes. Roll it out into two round cakes, pinch them nicely round, and place the candied peel so that each piece when cut will hold one slice of peel in the centre. Bake in a quick oven for 15 to 20 minutes.

SWISS ROLL.

INGREDIENTS.

6 eggs.	A squeeze of lemon juice.
3 tablespoonsful pulverized sugar.	A small quantity of jam.
4 „ flour.	1 teaspoonful of baking powder.

METHOD.— Beat the yolks and whites of the eggs separately to good froth in dry vessels with a wire whisk. Pour both together into a mixing bowl, beat again 10 minutes, adding sugar and flour gradually until all is mixed. Add 1 teaspoonful of baking powder just before putting it in the oven. Pour on to well larded paper on a pastry tin. Place it at the bottom of a moderate oven until set and risen. Then finish baking with top heat. Turn it on to a board, take off the paper, cover it with jam, roll up and leave it to cool before cutting.

SAVOURY OMELET.

INGREDIENTS.

3 eggs.	1 teaspoonful finely chopped parsley.
1 tablespoonful milk.	1 oz. butter.
1 saltspoonful salt.	A piece of onion the size of a pea, finely chopped.
1 saltspoonful pepper.	

METHOD.—Break the eggs, separating carefully the whites from the yolks ; put the yolks in a basin, the whites on a plate. Stir gently to the yolks, the salt, pepper, milk, parsley and onion. Add to the whites a small pinch of salt ; beat with a knife to a stiff froth ; add this to the yolks, stirring very little. Put the butter into a small clean frying pan. Melt, but do not brown it. Pour in the omelet ; set on the fire ; stir with a wooden spoon, bringing the cooked parts up and letting the uncooked parts get to the bottom. When it is all very lightly set, gather to one side of the pan ; slip a clean knife under every part of the omelet to be sure it does not stick ; turn it quickly but carefully quite over to the other side of the pan ; brown lightly. Turn out on to a hot plate and serve at once. Grated cheese, ham, tongue, or chopped kidney may be substituted for the parsley and onion.

MACARONI AU GRATIN.

INGREDIENTS.

6 ozs. macaroni.	2 tablespoonsful crumbs.
6 ozs. cheese.	$\frac{1}{2}$ teaspoonful salt.
2 ozs. butter.	Pepper, cayenne.
1 pint water.	

METHOD.—Break the macaroni into one-inch lengths, put it into a stew pan with the water and salt, and let it simmer slowly one hour. Then pour half of it into a pie dish, and sprinkle over it half the grated cheese, half the butter, and half the crumbs. Lay in the remaining macaroni, the other half of the cheese, butter, and crumbs, and bake in a sharp oven until it is brown, about 30 minutes.

ASPIC JELLY.

INGREDIENTS.

2 ozs. gelatine.	$\frac{1}{4}$ oz. peppercorns.
$\frac{1}{2}$ oz. salt.	Juice of one lemon.
Rind of one lemon.	$\frac{1}{4}$ pint malt vinegar.
2 bay leaves.	$\frac{1}{4}$ oz. celery seed or one stick of
2 teaspoonsful Tarragon vinegar.	celery.
1 onion.	Shells and whites of two eggs.
1 quart cold water.	

METHOD.—Steep the gelatine in the water till soft, add all the other ingredients, and whisk over a quick fire till it boils. Boil it without stirring for five minutes, then cover and stand to settle for five minutes. Pour some boiling water through a felt jelly bag, keeping the bag covered to retain the heat. As soon as the water is out, pour the jelly in, and when it begins to run clear, change the basin under the bag, and pour the first flow of the jelly back into the bag. Keep the bag covered and in a warm place. The jelly being stiff for garnishing will harden in the bag, and waste if allowed to become cool.

N.B.—In very hot weather $2\frac{1}{2}$ ozs. of gelatine will be required for this quantity.

HAM AND EGGS.

INGREDIENTS.

Ham.
2 eggs for each person.
1 to 2 ozs. lard.

METHOD.—To fry ham have pure lard very hot. Fry quickly. Eggs are always best fried in the same fat after the ham, providing the fat is not discoloured, or that there is no salt in the frying pan. Break the eggs one by one into a cup before placing in the frying pan; in this way a bad egg can never get mixed with the good ones. When eggs are old they are better scrambled than fried. Grilled ham and scrambled eggs can be served on the same dish.

RAW BEEF TEA.

INGREDIENTS.

½ lb. raw tender beef.
½ pint cold water.
1 saltspoon of salt.

METHOD.—Scrape the beef with a sharp knife until nothing is left but fibres. Cut through and scrape again until nothing remains but skin. Place the scraped beef in a basin with the cold water, and leave it standing for four hours, covered with paper. Stir it up occasionally. Strain and add salt before giving to a patient. If served in a coloured glass this beef tea looks less objectionable

EXTRA COURSE.

COCOA NUT SOUP.

INGREDIENTS.

2 quarts stock.	6 ozs. ground rice.
½ teaspoonful mace.	6 ozs. grated cocoa nut.
Pepper.	½ pint (mixed) condensed
Salt.	milk.

METHOD.—Add the ground rice, cocoa nut, mace, pepper, and salt to the stock. Simmer slowly for 1 hour. Strain through a hair sieve. Add the milk. Re-heat and serve.

CHANTILLY SOUP.

INGREDIENTS.

1 pint marrowfats, or any other good dried peas.	½ teaspoonful sugar.
	2 quarts stock.
2 small onions.	1 sprig mint.
½ bunch parsley.	Pepper, salt.

METHOD.—Soak the peas in cold water for 12 hours. When soft add them to the stock with the other ingredients, and boil it until the peas are quite tender, then rub the soup through a sieve. Re-heat it and season carefully before serving.

N.B.—This soup will be better if made with fresh or tinned peas, in which case the peas must be boiled in an uncovered pan in order to preserve their colour.

BAKED SOUP.

INGREDIENTS.

2 lbs. meat.	2 small onions
1 good sized carrot.	1 small turnip.
2 tablespoonsful rice.	2 quarts water.
1 teaspoonful chopped parsley.	Salt, pepper.

METHOD.—Cut the meat into four pieces, place them in a jar or stew pan with the water, vegetables cut small, rice and pepper. Cover the jar and bake for two hours. Remove the meat and the fat, stir in the chopped parsley and salt, and serve.

MILK SOUP.

INGREDIENTS.

2 quarts milk.	2 teaspoonsful sugar.
1 teaspoonful powdered	Yolks of 4 eggs.
cinnamon.	A few sippets of untoasted
½ teaspoonful salt.	bread.

METHOD.—Place the milk in a clean pan over the fire, add the sugar, salt, and cinnamon. Simmer slowly for 10 minutes. Beat the yolks, add them to the milk, and stir until the soup thickens. Put the bread into the tureen, pour the soup over, and serve.

OX-TAIL SOUP.

INGREDIENTS.

1 ox tail.	3 tablespoonsful dripping.
1 large carrot.	3 quarts stock.
1 onion stuck with 4 cloves.	½ bunch sweet herbs.
3 tablespoonsful flour.	Pepper, salt.

METHOD.—Joint the ox tail, wash well and dry the pieces. Melt half the dripping in a stew pan, put in the pieces of tail and the prepared carrot, cut small. Fry until browned—about 10 minutes. Add the stock, the onion stuck with the 4 cloves, bring to the boil, skimming well. Simmer for 2 hours, or until the tail is tender.

Take a second stew pan, melt in it the remainder of the dripping, add the flour, and fry until browned. Add gradually the strained stock from the ox tail. Boil up, and serve the pieces of tail in the soup.

SHEEP'S HEAD BROTH.

INGREDIENTS.

1 sheep's head.	2 quarts water.
1 onion.	1 small carrot.
½ bunch herbs.	2 cloves.
3 tablespoonsful barley.	Sprig of parsley.
Pepper, salt.	1 ham bone.

METHOD.—Split the head down the centre and remove the brains. Wash the head and steep it one hour in salt and water. Place the head and the ham bone in a stew pan with the water. Bring it to boiling point, skimming well. Add the barley and the herbs and cloves tied up in a piece of muslin. Simmer for 1½ hours, then add the carrot and onion cut small. Simmer for another half-hour. Take the bones from the head, remove the skin from the tongue, and serve the head with brain sauce sprinkled with chopped parsley.

TWICE LAID (COLD FISH AND POTATOES.)

INGREDIENTS.

1 lb. cold fish, fresh or salt.	¼ teaspoonful pepper.
2 lbs. cold potatoes.	1 teaspoonful anchovy sauce.
1 small onion.	Salt to taste.
1 teaspoonful mustard.	

METHOD.—Bone the fish, and mince it finely. Boil and mince the onion, add it to the potatoes, fish, onion, sauce, and the other ingredients, mash well together and fry in a hot greased frying pan in a large cake, brown both sides, and garnish with parsley.

OYSTER FRITTERS.

INGREDIENTS.

20 oysters.
20 thin rashers fat bacon.
Pepper.

METHOD.—Place an oyster on each piece of bacon. Sprinkle them lightly with pepper, and roll them up firmly. Run a skewer through the rolls, and bake them in a quick oven for 15 minutes.

CURRIED LOBSTER.

INGREDIENTS.

1 tin lobster.	1 teaspoonful vinegar.
1 tablespoonful butter.	½ ,, sugar.
1 ,, curry powder.	½ pint water.
1 dessertspoonful flour.	Cayenne pepper.

METHOD.—Heat the butter in a stew pan. Add the curry powder and flour, mix smooth and cook for one or two minutes. Add the water gradually, when it boils put in the cayenne, vinegar, sugar and the lobster with its liquid. Heat through without boiling. Serve with dry boiled rice.

MEAT AND POTATO PIE.

INGREDIENTS.

1 lb. beef or mutton.	1 teaspoonful of flour.
1 lb. potatoes.	¼ pint cold water.
1 small onion.	Salt to taste.
¼ teaspoonful of pepper.	

METHOD.—Cut the meat and potatoes rather small. Mix the pepper, salt and flour, then slightly coat the meat with it. Place it in a small pie dish, add the onion sliced, and put the potatoes over all. Add the water and cover with crust.

FOR CRUST.

6 ozs. flour.	A little cold water.
2 ozs. dripping.	A pinch of salt.

Mix the flour and salt, break the dripping in pieces the size of peas into the flour, and mix it to a light dough with the water. Roll out once only a little larger than the pie dish, cut off the outer edge. and line the dish all round with the strips. Brush over with a little water, cover, decorate and ventilate. Bake 40 minutes in a quick oven.

CURRIED CHICKEN.

INGREDIENTS.

1 good sized chicken.	1 teaspoonful salt.
1 tablespoonful curry powder.	1 good sized potato or 1 green
1 tablespoonful butter or good	apple.
dripping.	½ pint water.
1 tablespoonful grated cocoa	1 teaspoonful vinegar.
nut.	½ teaspoonful sugar.
1 dessertspoonful flour.	

METHOD.—Cut the chicken in joints, and brown them without burning in a little hot fat. Place the butter in a clean stew pan, make it hot, and fry the finely cut onion in it. Remove the onion, and add the flour and curry powder, stir until it becomes a paste, and let it simmer for a few seconds, then add the water gradually, keeping it well stirred. Return the chicken, onion, and all the other ingredients, and simmer for 40 minutes, keeping it closely covered.

KEGEREE.

INGREDIENTS.

1 lb. cold fish.	½ lb. Patna rice.
2 tablespoonsful butter.	1 teaspoonful mustard.
2 hard-boiled eggs.	Salt, cayenne.

METHOD.—Boil the rice and dry it. Bone and flake the fish, and mix all the ingredients together, the eggs being cut in eight pieces. Decorate with sprigs of parsley. Serve very hot.

BEEF STEAK PIE.

INGREDIENTS.

2 lbs. tender steak.	¼ teaspoonful salt.
⅙ lb. puff paste.	¼ teaspoonful pepper.
1 hard boiled yolk.	¼ pint water.
1 teaspoonful flour.	

METHOD.— Cut the steak into thin fillets, two inches long, leaving a little fat on each side. Mix together the flour, pepper and salt, and dip each fillet into the mixture. Roll them up and place in a pie dish, add the yolk of egg cut into four pieces. Fill the dish with the meat, leaving the centre slightly raised. Half fill the dish with water. Line the edges with pastry, cover the pie with the rest of the paste, and decorate nicely, making a hole at each end of the pie to let out the steam. Bake in a quick oven until the paste is cooked, then the meat can be cooked more thoroughly by leaving the dish on the range for about 40 minutes.

STEWED GIBLETS.

INGREDIENTS.

2 lbs. giblets.	2 tablespoonsful flour.
4 cloves.	2 small onions.
1 teaspoonful salt.	½ teaspoonful white pepper.
½ „ thyme.	1 pint water.
2 tablespoonsful dripping.	

METHOD.—Cut the giblets into rather large pieces, leaving out the liver, fry them brown in hot fat. Place the dripping in a stew pan, make it hot, and in it fry the onions, cut small, allow them to brown. Remove them and brown the flour, add the water gradually, then add the giblets, onions, cloves stuck into a piece of carrot, season, and simmer for 1½ hours, keeping it well covered.

COLLARED BEEF.

INGREDIENTS.

6 or 8 lbs. of the thin end of flank.	2 tablespoonsful chopped parsley.
2 ozs. sugar.	1 bunch mixed herbs.
1 oz. saltpetre.	1 teaspoonful mixed spice.
6 ozs. salt.	

METHOD.—Prick the meat all over with a wooden skewer, and rub it well with the salt, sugar, and saltpetre. Place it in a harness cask for four days, every day turning and rubbing it with dry salt. Before cooking remove the bones and wipe the meat dry, sprinkle it with the chopped parsley, herbs, and spice, and roll it up firmly, fasten it together with wooden skewers, and bind it together with tape or twine. Boil slowly for five hours. Trim neatly, change the skewers and remove the tape when the meat is cold. To be served cold.

FRICANDEAU OF BEEF.

INGREDIENTS.

3 lbs. fillet of beef or rump.	2 bay leaves.
4 cloves.	1 glass sherry.
1 pint stock or water.	1 bunch of herbs.
¼ teaspoonful spice.	Bacon for larding.
Pepper and salt.	

METHOD.—Cut some firm, fat bacon into thin strips, 1¼ in. long and rather more than ⅛ in. thick. Insert the strips into a larding needle and lard the beef. Put it into a stewpan with the stock, sherry, and other ingredients. Cover the pan and simmer for two hours. Remove the meat from the pan. Skim off the fat from the gravy and strain it. Boil the gravy to a glaze, and pour over the meat. Serve with sorrel sauce.

BULLOCK'S HEART ROASTED.

INGREDIENTS.

1 heart.	Forcemeat.

METHOD.—Wash the heart well after cutting away the lobes. Wipe it dry and fill it up with the well-seasoned forcemeat. Cut a crust of bread and place it over the forcemeat and fasten with a skewer to keep the forcemeat in its place. Bake, keeping it well basted with plenty of dripping, for 2 hours.

FORCEMEAT.

INGREDIENTS.

¼ lb. cold beef or mutton.	1 sprig parsley.
¾ small onion.	½ teaspoonful dried herbs.
1 oz. bread.	A little spice, cayenne, salt.

METHOD.—Soak the bread, squeeze it dry. Chop the meat and onion very finely, and mix all the ingredients well together. If wanted for forcemeat balls, this mixture can be bound together with the yolk of an egg, or with a little flour.

PIGEON PIE.

INGREDIENTS.

1 lb. tender steak.	3 eggs, 2 ozs. butter.
3 pigeons.	1 teaspoonful flour, pepper, salt.
½ lb. sliced ham.	½ lb. puff paste.

METHOD.—Rub the pigeons inside and out with butter, sprinkle them with pepper, salt, and flour. Lay the steak cut in thin two-inch fillets at the bottom of a pie dish, and season with pepper, salt, and flour. Lay the pigeons in, with a piece of bacon on the breast of each pigeon, add the hard boiled yolks of eggs cut in quarters, and half fill the dish with water.

Lay a border of paste round the edge of the dish, wet it and cover loosely to allow for shrinking during process of baking. Ornament the top edge. The feet (which must previously have been scalded and skinned) should project through the hole in the centre of the crust. Glaze the crust with egg and bake in a moderate oven for 1½ hours.

FRICASSEED CHICKEN.

INGREDIENTS.

1 large chicken.	1½ tablespoonsful flour.
2 ozs. butter.	½ teaspoonful pepper.
½ bunch fresh parsley.	½ pint stock or water.
1 small onion.	Salt.
Juice of ½ lemon, or	A little nutmeg.
1 teaspoonful lime juice.	Yolks of 2 eggs.

METHOD.—Cut the chicken into joints, skin them, wash, wipe dry, and dust them with a little flour. Make the butter hot, add the flour and stir well, preventing it from browning. Add the stock or water gradually, keeping it well stirred. Add the chicken, parsley, sliced onion, pepper, and salt, and simmer until the fowl is tender. Remove the parsley and onions, and add seasoning. Whip the yolks of the eggs, and stir them in with the lemon or lime juice just before serving. It must not boil after the eggs are added.

BEEF À LA MODE.

INGREDIENTS.

6 lbs. neck of beef in one piece.	1 lb. of bacon.
2 good sized carrots.	Pepper and salt.
2 tablespoonsful piccalilli.	2 tablespoonsful dripping.
4 small onions.	2 tablespoonsful flour.
2 bay leaves.	1 pint water.
6 cloves.	

METHOD.—Cut, peel, and wash one carrot, and cut the bacon into two pieces, thick, long, and square. Run a knife through the beef with the grain. Force the carrot and bacon through the cuts and trim the ends off level with the beef. Place the beef in a hot oven for one hour, dredging it with flour and basting it with hot fat. Place the dripping in a large stewpan, make it hot, brown in it the flour, then gradually add the water to form the gravy. Add the remaining carrot (cut into pieces the size of a chestnut), the onions whole, with cloves, bay leaves, pepper, salt, and piccalilli. Lay in the beef, and simmer for 2¼ hours. Serve the vegetables and gravy round the joint.

PILLAU OF FOWL.

INGREDIENTS.

1 fowl.	Cayenne.
2 ozs. butter.	A little mace and cinnamon.
6 thin slices bacon.	Salt.
2 hard boiled eggs.	1 lb. rice.
2 tablespoonsful of raisins.	1 teaspoonful allspice.
2 quarts stock.	Pepper.
8 cloves.	

METHOD.—Place the butter in a stew pan to become hot, throw in the raisins after removing the stones; when these are swollen and round like a grape, take them out and add the rice (after washing it well), and brown it, keeping it well stirred.

Tie the spices and herbs up in muslin, and put them with the fowl in the stock, and simmer for 20 minutes. Then put the stock and the fowl in the pan of rice, add a skewer of cayenne, cover closely, and simmer slowly one hour. If the stock is not dried up, uncover the pan during the last ten minutes.

Take out the fowl, cut it into eight pieces, and pile them up in the centre of a large dish, cover well with the rice, and decorate it with the eggs cut in quarters, the raisins, bacon, and the fried onions.

BUBBLE AND SQUEAK.
(Cold Meat Cookery.)

INGREDIENTS.

2 lbs. cold vegetables.	1 small onion.
½ lb. bacon.	Pepper, salt.
½ lb. cold beef.	1 tablespoonful butter.

METHOD.—Chop the vegetables rather finely, slice the onion and brown it in hot butter. Remove the onion, and fry the bacon cut into 8 small pieces. Fry the beef lightly in the same way. Lay the slices of beef in the bottom of the dish, place the bacon on the top. Season the vegetables, and fry them in the butter, lay them on the beef and bacon, sprinkle over them the fried onions, and serve very hot.

RAGOUT OF FOWL.
(Cold Meat Cookery.)

INGREDIENTS.

Remains of cold fowl.	½ bunch thyme.
1 small onion sliced.	1 pint water.
2 blades mace.	2 slices lean ham.
3 cloves.	Squeeze of lemon juice.
1 tablespoonful butter.	Pepper, salt, pinch of sugar.
1 tablespoonful flour.	

METHOD.—Cut the fowl into joints the same as for a Fricassee. Place the trimmings in a stew pan, with the water, onion, mace, herbs, cloves, pepper and salt, and simmer for 20 minutes.

Make the butter hot in a stew pan, brown it in the flour. Strain the stock, and add it gradually to the flour and butter, and make a rich gravy. Place the fowl in this for the last 10 minutes, with the lime juice. Serve with the ham cut in small fillets round the dish.

TOAD IN THE HOLE.
(Cold Meat Cookery.)

INGREDIENTS.

½ lb. cold mutton.	1 pint milk.
3 or 4 mutton kidneys.	2 large eggs.
6 tablespoonsful flour.	Pepper, salt.

METHOD.—Beat the eggs lightly and add the milk and flour and beat for ten minutes. Place the kidneys cut small and the well-seasoned cold mutton in a buttered pie dish. Pour over this the batter, and bake for 1¼ hours in a moderate oven. Send to table in the same dish with a serviette round the edge.

FRUIT AND CUSTARD.

INGREDIENTS,

1 bottle cherries.	8 tablespoonsful sugar.
1 pint milk.	3 eggs.

METHOD.—Put half of the juice from the cherries into a stewpan, with five tablespoonsful of sugar; boil it down to a good syrup, and pour it when cold over the cherries.

Beat the eggs and milk with the rest of the sugar, pour it into a well-buttered basin, cover it with buttered paper, and bake slowly in an oven until the custard is firm. When cool turn it out on to the centre of a large glass dish, and pour the cherries and syrup around.

APRICOT SOUFFLÉE.

INGREDIENTS.

2 lb. tin of apricots.	2 tablespoonsful corn flour.
6 eggs.	½ pint milk.¦ ½ lb. sugar.

METHOD.—Strain the apricots from the juice, and rub them through a wire sieve. Stir the milk, corn flour, sugar, and fruit over the fire, and boil for five minutes. Add the yolks (which must first be separated from the whites), and mix well. Add the stiffly whipped whites, mixing them in lightly but thoroughly. Pour into a buttered mould, and bake in a hot oven for 20 minutes.

BACHELOR'S PUDDING.

INGREDIENTS.

4 ozs. bread crumbs.	3 eggs.
4 ozs. currants.	6 drops essence of lemon.
4 ozs. finely-chopped apples.	A pinch of spice.
2 tablespoonsful sugar.	

METHOD.—Mix all the dry ingredients thoroughly. Beat the eggs, pour them into the mixture, add the essence, and beat well. Put it into a buttered mould, and cover with buttered paper. Steam for 2½ hours. Serve with sweet lemon sauce.

MILITARY PUDDING.

INGREDIENTS.

½ lb. bread crumbs.	Rind and juice of 1 lemon, or
6 ozs. suet.	2 tablespoonsful of lime juice.
6 tablespoonsful moist sugar.	½ pint of milk, 1 egg.

METHOD.—Chop the suet finely, add the crumbs, sugar, grated lemon rind, and juice. Mix well, make into a firm mixture by the addition of the beaten egg and milk, place in a buttered mould and steam for 2 hours. Serve with lemon sauce.

MARLBOROUGH PUDDING.

INGREDIENTS.

4 eggs.	¼ lb. butter.
¼ lb. fine white sugar.	¼ lb. jam.
4 tablespoonsful flour.	½ lb. puff pastry.

METHOD.—Line the pie dish with the puff pastry. Lay in the jam. Beat the eggs, butter, sugar, and flour to a light batter. Pour it over the jam. Bake one hour in a moderate oven.

BAKEWELL PUDDING.

INGREDIENTS.

¾ pint bread crumbs.	3 ozs. butter.
1 pint milk.	10 pounded almonds.
3 eggs.	½ lb. jam.
3 ozs. sugar.	

METHOD.—Put the crumbs into a buttered pie dish, and over them a layer of jam. Beat the eggs, add the milk, sugar, and almonds. Pour this mixture over the jam, and bake for one hour in a moderate oven.

CUSTARD PUDDING.

INGREDIENTS.

¾ pt. milk.	A little spice.
8 eggs.	Puff pastry.
4 tablespoonsful sugar.	Rind of ½ a lemon.
1 oz. butter.	

METHOD.—Heat the milk, sugar, and lemon rind. Leave it for 20 minutes to extract the lemon flavour. Beat the eggs, strain the milk to them, stirring well. Add the butter and spice, and pour into a pie-dish lined around the edge with puff paste. Bake ¾ of an hour in a slow oven.

APPLE SNOWBALLS.

INGREDIENTS.

6 apples.	½ lb. rice.
1 pint milk.	8 cloves.
3 dessertspoonsful sugar.	

METHOD.—Peel and core the apples, place one clove and a little sugar in the centre of each. Wash the rice, and boil it for ten minutes in the sweetened milk. Strain the rice, and cover each apple with it. Tie each ball in a piece of muslin. Boil gently until the apples are tender. Remove the muslin, and serve the snowballs in a glass dish, with coloured syrup poured over.

COMPASS PUDDING.

INGREDIENTS.

1 quart milk (fresh or condensed).	4 tablespoonsful white sugar.
5 tablespoonsful corn flour.	4 drops essence of almonds.
3 eggs.	A pinch of salt.

METHOD.—Make a smooth batter with the corn flour and milk. Stir over the fire until it boils. Remove from the fire, add half the sugar and the beaten eggs. Allow the eggs to cook but not to boil. Add the salt, also the essence. Have ready a pie-dish with nearly half of the sugar laid in the bottom. Pour in the custard, cover it with paper and allow it to cool. When cold, this pudding (being laid on the sweet liquid) will move, with the movement of the ship, like the compass.

ALMA PUDDING.

INGREDIENTS.

¼ lb. flour.	3 tablespoonsful currants.
½ lb. powdered sugar.	¼ lb. butter. 4 eggs.

METHOD.—Wash the salt out of the butter, squeeze it dry in a clean cloth. Beat the butter and sugar to a cream. Add the eggs and flour alternately, beating well. Add the currants (which must be washed and dried). Pour into a buttered mould, cover with a buttered paper. Steam for three hours. Serve with gooseberries and syrup.

SWEET BATTER PUDDING.

INGREDIENTS.

1 pint milk.	3 tablespoonsful flour.
3 eggs.	A pinch of salt. A few
1 oz. butter.	drops essence of lemon.
2 tablespoonsful sugar.	

METHOD.—Make a batter of the flour, milk, and eggs, and beat it for 15 minutes, slightly warm the butter, add it to the batter, also the salt and essence of lemon. Pour into a well buttered mould, cover with buttered paper. Steam for two hours. Serve with jam sauce.

CANARY PUDDING.

INGREDIENTS.

3 eggs, their weight in sugar and butter.	2 good tablespoonsful flour.
	Rind of one lemon.

METHOD.—Beat the butter and sugar to a cream, with the finely minced lemon rind. Add the flour and beaten eggs alternately. Beat well, and pour into a buttered mould. Cover with buttered paper, and steam for two hours. Serve with sweet sauce.

AMBER PUDDING.

INGREDIENTS.

6 apples.	3 ozs. butter.
¼ lb. white sugar.	3 eggs.
Rind and juice of 1 lemon.	A little castor sugar.
¼ lb. puff pastry.	

METHOD.—Butter the bottom of a pie dish. Line the edges with puff pastry and decorate them. Peel, core, and stew the apples to a pulp with the lemon rind, juice, and sugar. Rub them through a wire sieve, and add the beaten yolks. Mix thoroughly. Pour the mixture into the pie dish, and bake for 20 minutes in a moderate oven. Beat the whites to a stiff froth, add a little castor sugar, and pile them high on the apple mixture; return it to the oven until the whites are set and lightly browned.

PLAIN CABINET PUDDING.

INGREDIENTS.

2 ozs. stoned raisins.	A few slices thin bread and
2 eggs.	butter.
1 pint milk.	Sugar, and a little nutmeg.

METHOD.—Butter a pudding mould and decorate it with the raisins. Cut the bread (buttered) into even shapes, and line the mould with it without disturbing the raisins. Beat the eggs, add the sugar, milk, and nutmeg. Pour this into the mould, and add sufficient bread to fill it. Cover with buttered paper, and steam for 2 hours. Serve with sherry sauce.

DELHI PUDDING.

INGREDIENTS.

6 large apples.	¼ teaspoonful grated nutmeg.
½ lb. cleaned currants.	Rind of 1 lemon minced fine.
1½ lbs. suet crust.	4 tablespoonsful white sugar.

METHOD.—Roll out the pastry as for a roll jam pudding. Cut the apples into thin small pieces, lay them over the pastry and sprinkle with the currants, sugar, lemon, and nutmeg. Slightly wet the edges, roll up evenly, fasten the ends, and tie the pudding up in a cloth wrung out of boiling water and floured. Steam for 2 hours. Serve with sweet sauce.

COLLEGE PUDDINGS.

INGREDIENTS.

1 pint bread crumbs.	3 tablespoonsful white sugar.
4 ozs. finely chopped suet.	3 eggs.
8 thin slices candied peel.	1 glass brandy or sherry.
3 tablespoonsful washed and dried currants.	$\frac{1}{4}$ teaspoonful nutmeg.

METHOD.—Mix together all the dry ingredients. Moisten them with the beaten eggs and brandy. Roll the mixture into balls of uniform size and fry them in hot lard, not too quickly. Place in the oven on paper for a few minutes to soak through. Serve with port wine sauce.

BAKED HAM.

Soak the ham all night in salt water, clean the parts that have no skin, wipe it dry. Cover it with a dough made of flour and water, and bake it rather slowly for four hours. Remove the crust, draw off the rind and crumb the ham. Serve hot or cold.

MAYONNAISE OF FOWL.

INGREDIENTS.

1 cold roast fowl.	3 hard boiled eggs,
3 young lettuces.	$\frac{1}{2}$ pint mayonnaise sauce.

METHOD.—Cut the fowl into joints. Pile them in the centre of a dish. Pour over them the mayonnaise sauce, and garnish with the hard boiled eggs in rings of white and rounds of yolks, with lettuce shredded and placed around.

TO MELT AND CLARIFY FAT.

All pieces of fat not likely to be eaten are best trimmed neatly off before meat is cooked, and put carefully aside to be melted. Fat remaining from cooked joints may also be used. Cut up the fat into pieces about $\frac{1}{2}$ an inch square and put into a shallow stew pan, do not put on the lid, just cover with cold water and bring to a boil.

A good deal of scum will rise as it comes to boiling; this must be carefully removed; a very moderate heat only must be allowed, as the water is only required to soften the animal tissue that the fat may come out more easily; and to remove impurities it is allowed to evaporate entirely.

Care must be taken that the fat does not burn; it must be kept over the fire until the scum looks dried up and *slightly* brown.

Draw it away from the fire to cool a little, then pour through a gravy strainer and set it aside for use. It should be quite white.

This answers for frying better than lard. It is excellent for pastry. Use in the proportion of 6 to 8 oz. to each lb. flour.

NOTE.—If not sufficiently cooled before straining, the fat will melt the strainer.

INDEX.

RECIPES.

SOUPS

SUNDRIES.

SUNDRIES—*continued.*